Charles H Picken

The Practitioners' Probate Manual

Containing Instructions as to Procedure in Obtaining Grants of Probate and

Administration

Charles H Picken

The Practitioners' Probate Manual
Containing Instructions as to Procedure in Obtaining Grants of Probate and Administration

ISBN/EAN: 9783337159122

Printed in Europe, USA, Canada, Australia, Japan

Cover: Foto ©Suzi / pixelio.de

More available books at **www.hansebooks.com**

THE PRACTITIONER'S

PROBATE MANUAL,

CONTAINING

INSTRUCTIONS AS TO PROCEDURE IN OBTAINING GRANTS OF PROBATE AND ADMINISTRATION,

WITH THE

RULES, ORDERS AND FEES,

AND

FULL DIRECTIONS AS TO THE PAYMENT OF

PROBATE AND ESTATE DUTY.

SEVENTH EDITION.

LONDON :
WATERLOW & SONS LIMITED,
LONDON WALL.

1897.

PRACTITIONER'S

PROBATE MANUAL.

Handbook to the Estate Duty,

CONTAINING

The Finance Acts, 1894 and 1896,

WITH A

LENGTHY COMMENT THEREON,

By ALFRED W. SOWARD

(Of the Legacy and Succession Duty Office, Somerset House).

SECOND EDITION.   IN CLOTH 5/- NET.

PREFACE TO SEVENTH EDITION.

————

THE demand for another edition of this work has afforded an opportunity to enlarge the same by adding a number of forms and amplifying the information given according to the most recent practice.

Special attention is called to the full directions given as to the preparation of the Affidavit for Inland Revenue and to the exhaustive particulars concerning the incidence of the Estate Duty contained in Chapter 3.

The new Rules relating to the sealing of English Grants in Ireland through the Principal Registry in London have been noted, as also is the recent practice as to second or subsequent grants. Instructions for the resealing of Colonial Grants have been added.

C. H. P.

October, 1897.

THE FINANCE ACT, 1894.

Waterlow & Sons Limited have prepared the following Forms for use <u>with the Inland Revenue Affidavits</u> issued under above Act.

No. 852.—Particulars of the Debts due and owing from the Deceased, being Part 1 of Schedule 1.

,, 852a.—Particulars of the money out on Mortgage, Bills, &c., comprised in Account No. 1.

,, 853.—Particulars of Real Property of which the Deceased was absolute owner, comprised in Account No. 5.

,, 854.—Particulars of the Debts and Incumbrances on the Real Property comprised in Account No. 5.

,, 854a.—Particulars of Personal Estate passing on the death of the Deceased included in Account No. 5.

,, 855.—Particulars of Real Property which passed on the death of Deceased under a disposition other than the Will of Deceased, comprised in Account No. 5.

,, 855a.—Particulars of Leasehold Property which passed on the death of Deceased under a disposition other than the Will of Deceased, comprised in Account No. 5.

,, 856.—Particulars of Leasehold Property, comprised in Account No. 1.

,, 856a.—Particulars of the Rents of Real and Leasehold Property, comprised in the Accounts.

,, 857.—Particulars of Stocks and Shares, comprised in Account No. 1.

,, 857a.—Particulars of "Other" property in respect of which Estate Duty is paid on separate Accounts.

Price 2d. each, 2/6 per quire,
PLUS POSTAGE.

WATERLOW & SONS LIMITED,
London Wall, London.

TABLE OF CONTENTS.

THE

PRACTITIONER'S PROBATE MANUAL.

CHAPTER 1.

PROBATES.

THE practitioner on receiving a will (with or without a codicil) for the purpose of proving the same should first consider the following points :—

1. Its execution.
2. Alterations or interlineations.
3. Plight and condition.
4. Incorporation by reference.
5. Appointment of executors.

1.—EXECUTION.

The attestation clause to a will or codicil should show (a) that it was signed by the testator, or by some other person in his presence and by his direction ; and such signature should be made or acknowledged by the testator in the presence of two or more witnesses present at the same time, and such witnesses should attest and subscribe the will in the presence of the testator. Should the attestation in the will be deficient in any of these points and there be a codicil, and such codicil show that the requirements of the Act have been complied with, and be on the same

(a) Wills Act, 1837, s. 9.

B

sheet of paper as the will, or on a separate sheet of paper
and the will referred to therein by date, no affidavit will be
required. If there be no such properly executed codicil,
an affidavit of due execution of the will will be required to
be made by one of the attesting witnesses to the will.
An affidavit made, in respect of the execution of a will, by
a witness who is also a witness to a codicil to such will,
should speak as to the execution of such codicil even if it is
properly attested. (*See* "Affidavit of Due Execution,"
p. 126.)

Will signed by direction of the Testator.—In this
case the attestation clause should show that the will was
read over to the testator and signed in his presence, and by
his direction, and that he acknowledged the signature made
for him in the presence of the witnesses. If this is not
shown in the attestation clause an affidavit of due execution
is required to be made.

Testator signs by his mark.—In this case the attestation clause must show that the will was read over to the
testator, and that he perfectly understood and approved
of its contents. If the attestation clause does not show
this, an affidavit will be required, to be made by a witness
or failing him by some person competent to speak to the
fact, to show that the testator had knowledge of the
contents of the will. Where such affidavit is made by one
of the subscribing witnesses, he must make the affidavit of
due execution in the usual form, with the following clause
added :—" And I lastly make oath that previously to the
execution of the said will by the said testator the same
was read over to him by me this deponent (or by *A. B.*
in my presence), and the said testator at such time seemed
thoroughly to understand and approve of the contents
of his said will."

Testator signs twice.—In this case it is necessary that an affidavit by one of the attesting witnesses be made explaining the circumstances of the double signature. If there appear to have been two or more attempts by the testator to sign, it sometimes becomes necessary to include in the affidavit the usual clause as to reading over and explanation.

Testator signs in the Attestation clause.— When (as is frequently the case in home-made or lithographed forms of wills) the testator signs in the attestation clause, an affidavit by one of the subscribing witnesses is required, to show that testator meant and intended such signature as his final signature to his will. (*See* "Affidavit of Due Execution," p. 126.)

Testator signs below the Witnesses.—When the signature of testator appears below the signatures of the witnesses, the supposition is that the testator signed after the witnesses, and this fact would render the will invalid. In order, therefore, to validate the will, an affidavit should be made by at least one of the witnesses, showing that testator signed first, and setting out fully the circumstances under which his signature appears below the signatures of the witnesses. If on affidavit of both witnesses being produced it should appear that the requirements of the statute (*a*) were not complied with, the Registrar will refuse probate. (*See* "Probate Refused," p. 116.)

Affidavits by attesting Witnesses.—Rule 70 says that : "In every case where an affidavit is made by a subscribing witness to a will or codicil, such subscribing witness shall depose as to the mode in which the said will or codicil was executed and attested."

(*a*) 1 Vic. c. 26 and 15 Vic. c. 24.

Attesting Witnesses dead.—When both the subscribing witnesses are dead, an affidavit should be made by some person present at the execution, and such person must depose to the death of the witnesses and to the facts of the execution, adhering to the usual form of affidavit of due execution as much as possible. In default of such affidavit, an affidavit as to the handwriting of deceased and of the attesting witnesses should be furnished and a statement that the witnesses are dead and that, as far as can be ascertained, no other person was present at the execution should be embodied. The Registrar will not refuse this affidavit if made by a person interested in the will. (*See* also p. 130, Rule 7.)

2.—ALTERATIONS OR INTERLINEATIONS.

When alterations, interlineations, or erasures appear in a will and are not authenticated (1) by the initials or signatures of testator and witnesses, in the margin, or (2) by a full reference to such alterations, etc., in the attestation clause, the ordinary affidavit as to execution will be required, and at the foot thereof the following clause should be added :—" And having particularly observed the following alterations appearing in the said will, namely (here recite alterations, giving the number of the line and page of the will in which they appear), I lastly make oath that such alterations as aforesaid were made and written in the said will as the same now appear previously to the execution thereof by the said testator." If the alteration is in the date of the will the deponent must in his affidavit indicate the circumstances which enable him to fix the date. If such attesting witnesses cannot make the required affidavit, an affidavit must be made by some person who can depose as to the time when such alterations were made, and if this evidence is not available an affidavit as to the facts must be filed. (For "Affidavit as to alterations," *see* p. 125.) If such alterations were made after the execution, and unattested, the probate will issue as if such alterations had not been made. In the latter case a copy of the will as it originally stood will be required to be made for registrar's fiat, and filed with the original will. (*See* "Fiat," p. 115, and Rules 8-11.)

3.—PLIGHT AND CONDITION.

If, from the appearance of the will, it appears that there may have been some document attached to it, or that some portion of it may have been cut off, the Registrar may call for an affidavit, to be made by the executors, or some other competent person, stating that the will was in the same plight and condition as when executed. If the affidavit is made by one of the subscribing witnesses, such witness will first depose to the execution of the will in the usual form. (*See* affidavit of "Plight and Condition," p. 131, and Rule 14.)

4.—INCORPORATION BY REFERENCE, etc.

When the testator by his will refers to any document *existing* at the date of the will, as containing a disposition of any part of his property, the opinion of the Registrar should be taken as to whether or not such document is to be incorporated with the original will and form part of the probate. If the will or codicil refers in error to some other testamentary disposition, *e.g.*, a codicil referring to the *three* previous codicils when in fact there were only two; an affidavit of search by the executors will be required.

5.—APPOINTMENT OF EXECUTORS.

Particular care should be taken that the names of the executors are correctly quoted in the will. Any discrepancy that may appear should be cleared off in the oath. For instance—if the correct name of an executor be "Thompson," and his name appears in the will as "Thomson," he would be described in the oath as "Thompson (in the will written 'Thomson')." If, however, the difference between the names is such as to suggest the probability that a person other than the applicant is the person intended by the testator, an affidavit of identity must be prepared, and must show that it was testator's intention to appoint the applicant, and that there was at the date of the will no person answering in all particulars to the name and description of the person appointed by the will. This affidavit may be made by the writer of the will or by some disinterested person competent to speak to the facts, and the facts must be of such a character as to satisfy the Registrar that the deponent is the person intended by testator to act as executor. (For form *see* page 128.)

Executor according to the tenor.—When a testator does not expressly name any executor, but by direction to pay debts or otherwise charges a trustee or legatee with the duties of an executor, such person may take a grant of probate as "Executor according to the tenor of the will."

Executor resides abroad.—In this case a grant of administration with the will annexed will be made to the attorney of such executor appointed under a power executed by him for that purpose; but grant will not be given to the attorney of an executor resident abroad if another executor appointed by the will is in the United Kingdom, unless such other executor renounce probate. (*See* pages 100 and 137.)

Executor a Minor.—A grant in these cases may be made to the guardian of the executor for his use and benefit until he shall attain his majority. (*See* p. 59.)

GENERAL.

Draft of Will executed.—In this case it is necessary to file a special affidavit setting out the circumstances under which the draft was executed ; and an affidavit as to search is also required.

Certificate of delay.—When a period of three years has elapsed from testator's death to the time of application for a first grant, a certificate under the hand of the applicant is required, to be verified by the practitioner (or such certificate may be made by the practitioner solely as solicitor for the party applying for the grant), to show why the grant has not been sooner applied for, and also to show for what purpose the grant is required. In all cases it is necessary to give particulars and value of the estate, and where the property in respect of which the grant is required is a reversion which has fallen into possession, the dates of death of testators and of life tenants should be given. (*See* " Affidavit or Certificate of Delay," p. 132.)

Seven clear days must elapse from the date of death before a grant of probate may be made.

Will bears no date.—In this case an affidavit by at least one of the subscribing witnesses speaking as to execution and particularly as to the date of execution is required, and to identify the will in the affidavit, it may be referred to as beginning thus " ," ending thus " ." The deponent should in the affidavit give his reason for remembering the date of the execution. But if neither of the witnesses remember the date of the execution, then the required affidavit may be made by any other person who may have been present at such execution. The usual affidavit of search for any other will may also be required. (*See* "Affidavit of Search," p. 132.)

Where the Will bears more than one date, the date last given in the will is taken as *the* date of the will, and no affidavit is necessary to substantiate it.

Scotch Will.—If the will has been confirmed by a Commissary Court, a certified copy showing such confirmation will be accepted without proof of validity. If the will has been merely deposited and not confirmed a certified copy will be accepted on filing an affidavit, by a Writer to the Signet or by an Advocate, that the will is valid according to Scotch law and that the copy would be accepted in a Scotch Court. (The form is given on page 129.) The grant is *not* limited until the original is produced.

Will in the Welsh language must be translated by a competent person, either a clergyman or a solicitor (*not* the extracting solicitor), and an affidavit by the translator verifying such translation and stating his qualification must be filed. The original will must be marked by the person applying for the grant.

Isle of Man Will.—An authenticated copy under the Seal of the Manx Court including a copy of the Act of Probate is accepted. An affidavit of domicil or of British status is not required.

Will of British subject dying domiciled abroad.— By virtue of The Wills Act, 1861 (24 & 25 Vict., cap. 114), if the will is made *out of* the United Kingdom, it will be admitted to probate if it can be shown that such will was made in accordance with (1) the law of the place where the same was made, or (2) the law of the place where such person was domiciled when the same was made, or (3) the laws then in force in that part of Her Majesty's dominions where he had his domicil of origin.

If the will was made *in* the United Kingdom it is valid if the same be executed according to the law of that part of the United Kingdom where the same was made.

In every case an affidavit as to British status is required except where the deceased died domiciled in any of the Colonies brought within the Colonial Probates Act, 1892, by Order in Council. (*See* page 105.) The affidavit of validity may also be required. The forms of affidavit will be found on pages 129 and 131.

The following are the words of the statute :—

Section 1. Every will and other testamentary instrument made out of the United Kingdom by a British subject (whatever may be the domicile of such person at the time of making the same or at the time of his or her death) shall as regards personal estate be held to be well executed for the purpose of being admitted in England and Ireland to probate, and in Scotland to confirmation, if the same be made according to the forms required either by the law of the place where the same was made, or by the law of the place where such person was domiciled when the same was made, or by the laws then in force in that part of Her Majesty's dominions where he had his domicile of origin.

Section 2. Every will and other testamentary instrument made within the United Kingdom by any British subject (whatever may be the domicile of such person at the time of making the same, or at the time of his or her death) shall as regards personal estate be held to be well executed and shall be admitted in England and Ireland to probate, and in Scotland to confirmation, if the same be executed according to the forms required by the laws for the time being in force in that part of the United Kingdom where the same is made.

Foreign Will.—On application in England for probate to a foreign will, if a verified copy of such will and of the grant of probate by a foreign Court is produced, the Registrar will not require an affidavit that the will is valid according to the law of the country of which the deceased was a subject. If the copy is not accompanied by a copy of the Act of Probate or the foreign equivalent thereto an affidavit as to the validity of the will must be filed. This affidavit must be made by an advocate or other duly qualified legal person having a status in the foreign country equal to the English barrister-at-law, and who is conversant with the laws of the country of which the deceased was a subject. (The form is given on page 129.) If the documents are in a foreign language a translation of same duly certified by a notary public must be annexed to them. The foreign copy, *not* the translation, must be marked by the deponent and the commissioner. The above rules apply to the will of an English person who had become naturalized in a foreign country notwithstanding the will may be in English form and duly attested.

The oath and affidavit to lead a grant of probate will be explained in the following chapters.

It should be noted that the Registrars do not settle draft papers except in complicated cases, and then only when the applicant resides abroad or the application is for a second grant.

CHAPTER 2.

OATH FOR EXECUTORS.

As the oath for executors is practically the groundwork for a grant of probate, it cannot be too carefully prepared. In order to clear up the different points arising in it, and to make its preparation as simple as possible, the oath is given at length and the blanks will be explained numerically.

[*Oath—For an Executor.*]

In the High Court of Justice.

PROBATE, DIVORCE AND ADMIRALTY DIVISION.
(PROBATE.)

THE   REGISTRY.

IN the Goods of   deceased.

1 (or we) (¹)
make oath and say that   believe the paper writing hereto annexed and
marked by   (a)to contain the true and original last Will and Testament
(²)   of (³)   of (⁴)   deceased ;
who died (⁵) on the   day of   , 18   , at   that (⁶)
and that *I am* (⁷)   Execut   in the said will named, and that
                    will well and faithfully administer the personal estate and effects of the said
Testat   by paying h   just debts and the legacies contained in h   Will [and
two codicils], so far as the same shall thereto extend and the law bind
and that   will exhibit a true and perfect inventory of all and singular
the said Estate and effects, and render a just and true account thereof whenever
required by law so to do ; and that the gross personal estate and effects of the said
Testat   is of the value of (⁸)   and no more, to the best of
knowledge, information and belief.

Sworn by
at
on the   day
of   18 .

Before me,

(The deponents should sign as near to the foot of the oath as possible, in order to leave room for fresh jurat here, should it be necessary to have the oath resworn.)

A Commissioner for oaths.

(a) See marking exhibits, p. 40.

1. *Name and description, etc.*—Here insert names, residences and occupations of the executors, taking care that the name, address and description agree with that given in the will. (*See* Chapter 1, p. 6.) Should the executor have changed his address or occupation since the date of the will, his postal address and occupation at the time of making the oath should also be given.

A Clerk in Holy Orders is described as " The Reverend   of   , Clerk." The description " Vicar of   " or " Rector of   " cannot be considered as the residence of an executor, but his true place of abode must be first given, and the description referred to will follow the word " Clerk."

Executor described as " the younger."—Where an executor, being the son of the deceased, is described in the appointment as " the younger," such description need not appear in the oath ; but where an executor, *not being* the son of the deceased, is described in the will as " the younger," he must be described as such in the oath, or as " heretofore the younger," as the case may be. Otherwise an affidavit of identity will be required.

A Dissenting Minister may be described in the oath as " The Reverend   of   , Wesleyan Minister," or as the case may be.

Where the executors are " Bankers' Clerks," " Merchants' Clerks," " Solicitors' Clerks," etc., they must be so described.

A Mariner or Seaman should be described as " Master Mariner," or " Mariner in the Merchant Service," or as the case may be.

An Executrix can only be described as " Spinster,"
" Widow," or " Wife of   (here give name of
husband)." If the applicant is the widow of deceased,
she will be described as "   of   ,
widow, the relict of the deceased hereafter named."

Deponents affirm.—Where Executors object to take
an oath the words in italics " make oath and say " must be
struck through, and the following clause inserted, " do
solemnly, sincerely and truly declare and affirm."

2. Insert here " with a codicil thereto," or as the case
may be; the number of the codicils, if more than one, should
be given. If the Executor is sworn on a certified copy the
oath should read " to contain the true last will, &c."

As to marking the will, *see* p. 40.

3. *Name of deceased.*—The full Christian name and
surname of the deceased should be inserted here.

As a general rule the Registrars adopt the signature
of a testator as his name, although it differ from the
name as written in the heading of the will. In
case of a variance between the name of the testator
in the heading of the will and the name as signed
at the foot or end of it, and in case the former is the
more correct, the testator should be described by the name
he signs, the word "otherwise," followed by the name
given him in the will, being added. If the testator's
name is wrongly spelt in the will, and he sign his will
by his initials or by a mark, he should be described in
the probate by his correct name, the word "otherwise,"
followed by the name written in the will, being added.
If the testator is described in the will as the " elder," but
does not so subscribe himself, such description is not to be
inserted in the probate. If the testator is described in the
will as the " younger," but does not so subscribe himself,

he should, notwithstanding, be described in the probate as the " younger," or " heretofore the younger," as the case may be. If an *alias* is required to be set up an affidavit as to the necessity of same must be given. The affidavit must state fully the reasons for the *alias*, such as the existence of deeds in both names or as the case may be.

4. *Residence of testator.*—If testator's place of residence at the date of death does not correspond with that given in the will both addresses should be inserted thus "
of   formerly of   ."
The occupation of deceased will follow the residence.

A mariner or seaman should be described as "master mariner," or "mariner in the merchant service," or as the case may be.

A Testatrix will be described as "spinster," "widow," or " wife of   ."

5. *Date and place of death.*—The date and place of death should here be shown. If by reason of deceased being lost at sea, or for some other reason the fact of the death cannot be sworn to, application must be made on motion to the Court for leave to presume the death to have taken place on or since some fixed period. An office copy of the order of Court must be filed with the other papers when the application for grant is made and a fee of 2s. 6d. paid in respect thereof.(a) The form of words should follow

(a) As the expense of moving the Court for a grant of probate or administration in cases of presumed death, when the property for which a representation is required is of small amount, is felt to be excessive, it has recently, with a desire to reduce expense to the parties in these cases, been directed that when the property to be claimed by the executor or administrator by means of the grant does not exceed £100, the motion in Court for the grant shall in future be dispensed with, and the application for the same shall be made to the Registrars of the Principal Probate Registry, who will require such advertisements to be published, and call for such evidence as they may consider necessary, and order the grant to issue or take the directions thereon of one of the Judges of the Court in Chambers.

the Order, thus :— " who died on or since the   day of
, 18   , as appears by an Order of this Division of the High
Court of Justice, made the   day of   , 18   , at some
place unknown." A Declaration of the Personal Estate is
also required (p. 133) and in the case of Administration the
sureties must justify (p. 130). The *place* of death must be
given as " who died on the   day of   18   , at sea,
on board the British steamship   ." If deceased had
disappeared and the exact date of death cannot be given, the
oath should read " was last seen alive on the   day of
          18   , and was found dead on the   day of
18   , at   ."

If the application is made in the District Registry the
fixed place of abode and the name of the district should be
added after the date and place of death. (*See* " List of
Registries," p. 176.)

6. *Relationship of Executors to deceased.*—In
addition to the ordinary description of executors, if they
bear any relationship to the deceased, such relationship, if
given in any part of the will, should be inserted here
thus :—" That I am the [son *or* daughter *or* niece, *or as the
case may be*] of the said deceased." Occasionally it becomes
necessary to be even more particular in the description ;
as, for instance, when a testator appoints " my nephew
          , son of my late brother   ," *or*
" my brother-in-law," *or* " my wife's sister." In every case
the description should correspond with that given in the will.

(a.) Executor a Minor.—If an executor is shown
by the will (in any part of it) to have been a minor when
the will was made, and the will bears date within 21
years of the application for Probate, the following clause
should here be inserted : " That I, the said (name of minor),
attained the age of 21 years on the   day of
          , 18   ."

(b.) Wife executrix—but not appointed by name.
—Where deceased appoints his wife an executrix, but
does not mention her by name in the will, the following
clause should here be inserted : " That I, the said (*name
of relict*), was the lawful wife of the said deceased at the
date of his said will—to wit, on the   day of
, 18   ."

7. *The style of the executors* (of which the following
are some examples) is to be inserted here :—

       One male executor. .   . . The sole executor.
       All males . .   . .   . . The executors.
(*a*) One of the executors being
       dead the other proves . . The surviving executor.
(*b*) Power reserved to one and
       the other proves . .   . . One of the executors.
(*c*) One or more of the executors
       renounce the other proves One of the executors.
       A female . .   . .   . . The sole executrix.
       All females . .   . .   . . The executrixes.
       Partly male and partly female
       executors . .   . .   . . The executors.
       For executor according to
       the tenor . .   . .   . . *See* Chapter 1, page 6.
       The relict of the deceased
       executrix for life or widow-
       hood . .   . .   . . The executrix for life
                            (if I remain a widow).
       Executor as to part of the
       estate . .   . .   . . That I am the sole
                          executor in respect of
                          all the personal estate
                          of the said deceased
                          except personal estate
                          in the Colony of

(a.) Deceased executor.—If one of the executors is dead at the time application is made for the grant, it should be stated in the margin of the oath whether he died in the lifetime of the testator or survived him and is since dead.

(b.) When power reserved.—When application for probate is not made by all the executors, and the non-proving executor has not renounced, power must be reserved to him to take a similar grant, and a note to that effect should be inserted in the margin, thus:—" Power to be reserved to *A. B.* and *C. D.* (relationship as in the will, and in the case of females the status as ' widow,' ' spinster,' ' wife of   ' to be added), the other executors." Such non-proving executor can come in at any future time and take out a grant of double probate (*see* " Double Probate," Chapter 11) or may subsequently renounce. (*See* page 100.) If one of the executors is a minor at the time of application for a grant of probate, power is to be reserved to him to come in and prove on attaining his majority (by taking out a grant of double probate), and a marginal note should be made in the oath as follows: " Power to be reserved to *A.B.* (relationship to deceased if any) a minor, the other executor named in the will, when he shall attain the age of 21 years." A copy of the account, No. 1, must be filed with the papers.

(c.) Where one of the executors renounces, a statement to that effect should be inserted in the margin in this form : " *A.B.*, the other executor named in the said will, has renounced." (*See* " Form of Renunciation of Probate," p. 137.)

8. Here insert in figures the actual *gross* amount of the Personal Estate in England corresponding to the amount shown as the total of the Account No. 1 in the affidavit for Inland Revenue. Care must be taken to insert this amount

C

specially in cases under the Finance Act, 1894, where Real Estate is included in the affidavit. The amount of the Real Estate must not of course be inserted in the oath, as the Court of Probate has jurisdiction over Personal Estate only. The grant cannot be limited to the amount of the Personal Estate, which is dealt with by the will, but extends to all the Personal Estate situate in England of which deceased died possessed. If deceased died possessed of Personal Estate in Scotland the oath will take the form indicated on p. 134.

The Solicitor extracting the grant should mark at the head of the oath " Extracted by *A.B.*, solicitor of   ."

The oath, being now supposed to be in proper form and correct in every particular, should be read over by or to the applicant, who will then sign it (usual signature sufficient) ; and particular care should here be taken that the signature agrees with the name.

Deponent a Marksman.—Where the deponent makes his mark, such mark must be made in the presence of the Commissioner who administers the oath. (*See* also page 19.)

Alterations in oath.—Care should be taken that the Commissioner initials all alterations, and where two alterations occur in the same line the Commissioner will initial each alteration.

If an alteration is made by erasure, and upon such erasure words or figures are written, the Commissioner must write such words or figures in the margin and initial same.

If the oath is returned by the Registrar for additions or amendments, and it becomes necessary to prepare a fresh form, the form which had been previously examined must be returned to the Registrar for comparison.

JURAT.

The following Rules will be ample explanation of the mode of filling up the jurat.

" In every affidavit made by two or more deponents, the names of the several persons making the affidavit shall be inserted in the jurat, except that, if the affidavits of all the deponents is taken at one time by the same officer, it shall be sufficient to state that it was sworn by both (or all) of the above-named deponents."

" No affidavit, having in the jurat or body thereof any interlineation, alteration or erasure, shall be filed or made use of, unless the interlineation or alteration other than by erasure, is authenticated by the initials of the officer taking the affidavit, nor in the case of an erasure, unless the words or figures appearing at the time of taking the affidavit to be written on the erasure, are re-written and signed or initialed in the margin of the affidavit by the officer taking it."

It may be added, however, that where there is only one deponent, it is sufficient to say " sworn at, etc., etc." Unless the place where the oath is taken has been mentioned before in the oath, the county in which the place is situate should be shown in the jurat.

The word " affirmed " will be substituted for " sworn," if the deponent affirms.

Deponent a marksman, or blind, or illiterate.— If deponent is a marksman, or is blind, or illiterate, the following must be inserted in the jurat, before the words " before me,"—" this affidavit having been first read over to the said *A.B.*, who seemed perfectly to understand the same, and made *his* mark thereto in my presence."

The practice, which obtains in the other Divisions of the High Court, of a third person witnessing the mark of an illiterate person and being sworn thereto does not apply to the Probate Division.

Who may administer oaths—in England.—(1) The Principal Registrars; (2) District Registrars; (3) Surrogates at the commencement of the Court of Probate Act, 1857; (4) Commissioners for Oaths; (5) persons specially appointed to administer oaths in the registries.

The oath must not be administered by the Extracting Solicitor.

In Scotland and Ireland and the Colonies the oath may be sworn before any Judge, Notary Public or other person lawfully appointed to administer oaths.

Oaths sworn in foreign parts should be taken before a Notary or a British Consular Agent.

By the Customs and Inland Revenue Act, 1881, and the Finance Act, 1894, certain Inland Revenue officers are appointed to administer oaths in cases which pass through them to the Court.

CHAPTER 3.

AFFIDAVITS FOR COMMISSIONERS OF INLAND REVENUE.

THE duty payable on an application for Grant of Probate or Administration in respect of the personal Estate of a person dying *on or before the 1st August,* 1894, is **Probate Duty** and is chargeable, by virtue of the Customs and Inland Revenue, 1881, upon the Personal Estate passing under the deceased's will or intestacy.

The duty payable if the deceased died *after* the 1st day of August, 1894, is **Estate Duty** under the Finance Acts, 1894 and 1896, and is charged upon all property, real and personal, which passes either constructively or actually upon the death of the deceased and whether under his will or intestacy or any other title.

CUSTOMS AND INLAND REVENUE ACT, 1881.
(44 VIC., CAP. 12.)

The forms provided for the payment of Probate Duty under this Act are as follows:—

Form A.—For use where the deceased died *on or before* the 1st day of August, 1894, in all cases except those for which form B. is applicable.

This form is also used for second and subsequent grants where the deceased died on or before the 1st August, 1894.

Form B.—For use where deceased died on or before the 1st day of August, 1894, where the whole personal estate *wherever situate,* and without deducting debts (including mortgage debts on specific property created by the deceased) and funeral expenses, does not exceed £100, so that no stamp duty is payable, or when such estate does not exceed £300, and the fixed duty of £1 10s. is payable under Section 33 of the Act. The court fee is 15s. only.

Form E.—For payment of Temporary Estate Duty under the Customs and Inland Revenue Act of 1889.

In filling up these forms it should be noted that the duty is charged upon the value of the estate *at the date of the affidavit* and that all income on the property due at the date of death and accrued to the date of the affidavit should be brought into the account. The debts to be deducted in form "A" must not be voluntary debts expressed to be payable on the death of the deceased or payable under any instrument not delivered to the donee thereof three months before the death of the deceased; nor debts primarily payable out of Real Estate, except in cases where the devisee and the residuary legatee are one and the same person, in which case he may elect to deduct the debt against the Personal Estate. Where the deceased died domiciled abroad a deduction of debts is not allowed except where such debts are specifically charged against or recoverable out of any property included in the affidavit. The funeral expenses must not include the cost of mourning or tombstone or the cost of transferring the body to any distant place of interment.

The rates of duty are as follows :—

Above £100 and not above £500...£1 for every full sum of £50 or part of £50.

„ £500 „ „ £1,000...£1 5s. for every full sum of £50 or part of £50.

„ £1,000 ...£3 for every full sum of £100 or part of £100.

If the estate is over £10,000 the Temporary Estate Duty, being an additional duty of £1 for every full sum of £100 or part of £100, is chargeable thereon. (Form E above.)

FINANCE ACTS, 1894 & 1896.

(57 & 58 VIC., CAP. 30 ; 59 & 60 VIC., CAP. 28.)

The forms for the payment of Estate Duty are as follows :—

Form A-1.—For use in cases where the property *passing on the death* of a person dying *after* the 1st day of August, 1894, consists of (1) Real and Personal Estate of the deceased to which he was absolutely entitled ; (2) property in which deceased or any other person had an interest which ceased on the death of the deceased and upon which Estate Duty is payable ; (3) property which, under the terms of the Act, is deemed to pass on the death of the deceased. This form must not be used for cases under Section 16 (1) of the Act of 1894. (*See* form B-1.)

Form A-4.—For use in cases where the *only* property passing on the death of the deceased and chargeable with Estate Duty is the deceased's own personal property situate in the United Kingdom ; except where form B-1 is applicable.

If by the deceased's death any *other* property, under any title whatever, became chargeable with Estate Duty this form should not be used.

Form B-1.—For use in cases where application for grant is made under section 16 (1) of the Act. This section applies in cases where the whole of the estate, real and personal, in respect of which Estate Duty is payable on the death of the deceased, *exclusive of property settled otherwise than by the will of the deceased,* does not exceed the *gross* value of £500, no deduction being taken for debts (including mortgage debts on specific property created by the deceased) and funeral expenses. *Inter vivos* gifts, *donationes mortis causâ,* Nomination Policies effected by the deceased, and property of which the deceased and any other person were joint tenants, are not considered "settled property," and their value and the value of any other property chargeable with Estate Duty not strictly within the definition given in Section 22 (1 *h. & i.*) of the Finance Act, 1894, must be considered in calculating the amount of the estate.

Moveable property situate abroad must be considered in fixing the limit of £500 unless the deceased died domiciled abroad.

By the operation of Section 17 of the Finance Act, 1896, where the Estate is of the net value of over £100 but not exceeding £200 the duty payable is £1. In order to obtain the benefit of the Section form A-1 or A-4 must be used.

Form A-5.—For use *in every case* where an application is made for a second or subsequent grant in respect of property which came within the operation of the previous grant. The *unadministered* assets only should be included giving the value for same *as at the date of the affidavit.*

For particulars as to the "free mark," which must be obtained in every case, *see* p. 38.

For *cæterorum* and other grants in respect of estates not the subject of the previous grant the appropriate form of affidavit, as for an original grant, must be used and the value of the assets stated as at the date of death.

Charge of Duty.

Every item of property of whatever value which is chargeable with duty must be taken into account and included in the assets.

The value of the property upon which Estate Duty is payable is the value at *the date of death* of the deceased, and the income of the assets up to such date should be brought into account. The particulars required in the affidavit are indicated in the various paragraphs and special attention should be given same.

If any part of the Personal Estate is situate in Scotland or Ireland the separate values should be given in paragraph 4 of the affidavit in order that the domicile may be noted on the grant for resealing in Scotland; or that the certificate of payment may subsequently be obtained for the purpose of resealing in Ireland. (*See* also page 102.)

If the deceased died domiciled out of the United Kingdom it is not necessary to give particulars of the property of the deceased situate abroad.

With reference to paragraph 13 it is necessary to give particulars of all other property *passing* by the death of the deceased, which is chargeable with Estate Duty, such as the deceased's own free Real Estate, gifts *inter vivos*, real and leasehold property of which deceased was tenant for life Nomination Policies, donations *mortis causâ*, annuities provided by the deceased other than by his will, etc. Aggregable and non-aggregable property passing on the death of the deceased and liable to Estate Duty should be distinguished. In respect of any of this " other property " which is liable to aggregation the duty thereon may be paid upon the affidavit, or may be paid upon a separate account. If not paid upon the affidavit paragraph 14 should be struck out ; and, for the purpose of fixing the rate of duty particulars and values of the aggregable estate should not be included in accounts Nos. 4 and 5 but should be shown by a schedule annexed to the affidavit. This schedule should give short particulars of the disposition under which the property passes and should show the relationship of the beneficiaries to the tenant for life.

If deceased had a share only of any item brought into the affidavit it is necessary to show how he became possessed of such share, *i.e.*, by will or purchase (giving full particulars), and it should be stated whether he had any and if so what interest in the remaining share.

The Schedules annexed to the affidavit should be of the same size as a page of the official form and should be signed by the deponents. It is not necessary to have same marked as exhibits by the Commissioner.

The values of the various items included in the affidavit are not critically examined at the time the grant is taken. This examination is made by the officials of the Legacy Duty Office to whom the affidavit is forwarded after the grant has passed the seal. A copy of the affidavit cannot be obtained from the Controller of Legacy Duties except upon the written consent of the person who rendered such affidavit or of his legal personal representative.

The various accounts annexed to the affidavit will be explained in their order. It may be convenient to state with regard to the important question of aggregation that if the estate passing on the death of the deceased (exclusive of property *settled* otherwise than by the will of the deceased) does not exceed the net value of £1,000 such property is not to be aggregated with any other property but forms an estate by itself.

ACCOUNT No. 1.—In this account must be included all the free Personal Estate of the deceased.

The various items to be included are set out in the official form but all personal property of which deceased died possessed which may not be indicated in the account should be brought in. For example : Property on board of ships represented by Bills of Lading in this country, property *in transitu* to the United Kingdom at the date of death, property on the high seas, patents, copyrights, etc. Real Estate agreed to be sold by the deceased in his lifetime or to purchase which the deceased gave any option to a Lessee, (which option has been taken), must be brought into account. The Personal Estate of the deceased situated abroad should not be included in Account No. 1. The principal values of the various items must be brought into account and the basis upon which such principal value has been calculated should be shown. If any asset has been valued for the purposes of duty the original valuation must be filed and will not be given out again unless stamped, in which case a copy will be required.

Particulars of the mortgage, book and other debts, and of the interest thereon *due* at the death, and an apportionment of such income to date of death, should be supplied by schedules annexed to the account. If the nominal value of any debt due to the estate is not brought into account an explanation should be furnished and the parties should add an undertaking to account for the balance if subsequently received.

Published quotations, or brokers' certificates, or letters from secretaries of companies should be supplied as evidence of the value at the date of death of stocks and shares included in the account which are not quoted on the London Stock Exchange List. If the securities are quoted in the London List it is not necessary to supply any evidence of value.

The value of the stocks and shares quoted in a Stock Exchange List is arrived at by taking the average price of the actual business done on the day. If no business has been done the price accepted by the Commissioners is the price between the lower quotation and the medium of the two prices quoted. For example : If the stock is quoted 148—152 the value for Estate Duty is 149 the medium between 148 and 150. The forthcoming dividends on the shares are not to be included unless the stock is quoted *ex div*.

If the deceased died on a Sunday or on any day when the Stock Exchange was closed the price must be taken from the list of the day preceding.

Foreign Bonds, etc., payable to bearer or transferable in the United Kingdom should be included in this account.

Full particulars of the leasehold property included in the account, such as the term of the lease, the ground-rent, names of tenants, separate rentals, annual deductions, etc., must be given. The rules regarding allowances and the valuation of leasehold property are the same as those relating to Real Estate, as to which see *infra*. Any mortgage due from the deceased for which the leasehold property is the sole security may be deducted from the principal value. The principal value of the property upon which duty is payable is the full marketable value thereof, and a statement that such value is given should be added to the particulars.

The *value* of all interests in expectancy of which deceased died possessed should be included whether the duty on such interests is paid on the death of the deceased, or is deferred by virtue of Section 7 of the Finance Act, 1894, or is not payable on such interest. If Estate Duty is payable on the death of the deceased, on the *corpus* of the fund out of which such interest springs, duty is not also payable on the value of the interest in expectancy ; but the value of such interest must be considered in the aggregation of the estate passing on the death of the deceased for determining the rate of duty. If the *corpus* of the fund already forms part of the aggregated estate, the value of the interest must be deducted from the summary for the purpose of determining the rate and amount of duty.

Examples of Interests in Expectancy are as follows :—

(a) Interest expectant in property of which a person living at the date of death of the deceased was tenant for life.

>   The value of the interest is aggregable with deceased's own estate and the duty may be paid on the affidavit or may be deferred.

(b) Interest expectant in property of which deceased was tenant for life under a disposition *not* made by the deceased and the income of which property passes for life to some person *other* than the wife or husband or lineal issue or lineal ancestor of deceased.

> The *corpus* of the property is chargeable with Estate Duty on deceased's death but forms an " Estate by itself " and is not aggregable. The *value* of the interest is not also chargeable with duty, but it is to be aggregated with deceased's own estate and other aggregable property for determining the rate of duty.

(c) Interest expectant in property of which deceased was tenant for life under a disposition *not* made by the deceased and the income of which property passes for life to the wife or husband or lineal ancestor or lineal issue of the deceased.

(d) Interest expectant in property of which deceased was tenant for life under a disposition made by the deceased and the income of which property passes for life to some person living at the death of deceased.

(e) Interest expectant in property of which a person living at the date of death of deceased was tenant for life under a disposition made by the deceased *within* 12 *months of his death ; or* made at any other time if deceased reserved to himself a power of revocation.

> In the above cases (c) (d) and (e) the *corpus* of the property is chargeable with Estate Duty on deceased's death and is aggregable, but the value of the interest is not aggregable and duty on such value of the interest is not payable on deceased's death.

Deductions against value.—With regard to the debts which may be deducted, special attention is called to Section 7 of the Finance Act, 1894, and it should be noted that full particulars of each item must be given. Where the debt is for " money lent " or " bank over-draft " the date of the loan and the nature of the security should be given, and it should be stated whether the debt is legally recoverable, giving the facts of the case. The names and addresses of all creditors must be supplied. If there is a deficiency of Real Estate after deducting the mortgages thereon such deficiency should be included in this schedule as a deduction against Personal Estate.

The funeral expenses must be reasonable, and no allowance will be made for mourning or a tombstone. The funeral expenses of a married woman, which are in strictness payable by her husband (unless specially charged on her separate estate by her will), may be deducted. The foreign debts and funeral expenses of a person dying abroad but domiciled in the United Kingdom are as a rule allowed, but *see* " Soward's Estate Duty," 2nd edition, page 92.

Account No. 2.—This account should contain particulars of the Personal Estate situate abroad of which a person dying domiciled in the United Kingdom was possessed. Estate Duty is chargeable thereon by virtue of Section 2 (2), Finance Act, 1894. The Channel Islands and the Isle of Man are deemed to be included in the term " abroad " for the purpose of Estate Duty. Foreign bonds, shares or stock saleable or transferable in the United Kingdom should not be included in this account but should be accounted for in Account No. 1. The value of foreign patent rights should be included in this account. In the schedule to the account must be shown the debts due from the deceased to persons resident out of the United Kingdom but not including debts contracted to be paid in the United Kingdom or charged on property situate in the United Kingdom which have been deducted in the schedule to Account No. 1. The debts must have been incurred by the deceased for full consideration in money or money's worth wholly for deceased's own use and benefit. In this schedule deduction should also be taken against the principal value of the property included in the Account No. 2, of any duty payable in a foreign country (not a British possession) by reason of deceased's death in respect of such property situate in that country. The duty, which has actually been paid upon Personal Estate included in this account in a British possession to which Section 20, Finance Act, 1894, has been applied by Order in Council, is allowed against the duty paid in England upon such property. If the section has not been applied to the possession the duty is treated as if paid in a foreign country, *see supra*. There is no provision in the Act for an allowance in cases where duty has been paid in a British Consular Court on the Personal Estate included in this account, but an application to the Treasury for an allowance will be considered. A deduction against such principal value may be taken of any sum, not exceeding 5 per cent. on the value of the property, representing *additional expense* incurred in administering or realizing such property by reason of the property being situate out of the United Kingdom. The ordinary expense of realization is not a proper deduction against Estate Duty, and therefore the amount to be taken must be only such extra expense entailed by reason of the situation of the property.

ACCOUNTS NOS. 3A AND 3B.—Particulars should be given in these accounts of the personal property, *other than that included in accounts Nos. 1 and 2*, of which the deceased was at his death competent to dispose but of which he did not dispose. A person is deemed competent to dispose of property if he had such an estate or interest therein or such general

power as would if he were *sui juris* enable him to dispose of
the property. In the second part of the account should be
given particulars of money which the deceased had at his
death a general power to charge on Real Property other than
his own Real Estate whether such power was exercised by his
will or not. Full information of the disposition by virtue of
which the deceased had power to dispose of the Personal
Property or to charge Real Property should be furnished;
such as the dates of deeds, names of parties thereto, name of
testator, date of death, date and place of proof of will, etc.

The accounts should only be used if the duty on the property included therein is being paid upon the affidavit and then
only if such property is liable to aggregation. If the duty is
not being paid upon the affidavit or the property is not aggregable, the value of the property should be shown by separate
schedules and referred to in paragraph 13 of the affidavit.

ACCOUNTS NOS. 4 AND 5.—In these accounts should be
included all *other* property chargeable with Estate Duty on
the death of the deceased and upon which duty is being paid
upon the affidavit for grant. Such "other property" includes
gifts *inter vivos*, donations *mortis causâ*, annuities provided by
deceased *other* than by his will, Real and Personal Estate of
which deceased was tenant for life, deceased's severable share
of property of which he was a joint owner, deceased's own
Real Estate, etc., etc. Leasehold property of which deceased
was the absolute owner must be included in Account No. 1
being part of his own Personal Estate.

The various items included in the account should be shown
by separate schedules, but the totals should be inserted in the
account on the form. In the case of property of which
deceased was tenant for life only, particulars of the disposition
under which the property passed and the relationship of the
beneficiaries to the deceased should be given. If deceased's
interest in any property was less than the whole a statement

showing how deceased acquired such interest should be annexed.

The principal value of each item should be given and the basis of such value must be indicated. In the case of real and leasehold property each item should be separately specified and numbered and the names of tenants and separate rentals supplied. If the property is unoccupied or is in the occupation of the owner or a relative the *gross* property-tax assessment, or if not so assessed the *gross* poor-rate assessment must be given. The *reduced* assessment for collection of Income Tax on the property is not accepted as an indication of the annual value of property for the purpose of Estate Duty. The annual deductions in respect of each item of the property should be stated in order to show the net annual value. The amount usually allowed for repairs is 10 per cent. on the gross annual value, but in the case of small property 15 per cent. is sometimes allowed on a statement as to the character of the houses. For agricultural property 7½ per cent. on the gross annual value is the usual allowance. Rates *paid by the owners* (and stated so to be) will be allowed, except in cases where the property-tax or poor-rate assessment is given as the gross annual value. Property-tax is not a proper deduction and no allowance is made against the annual value for empties or for expenses of collection. The interest on any mortgage charged on the property should not be taken into consideration in fixing the net annual value as the principal will be allowed against the saleable value.

The principal value upon which duty is payable is the price which the property would realize if sold in the open market. If the property has been sold since the death the *gross* amount realized is the basis for duty. In estimating the value of a freehold public-house the goodwill and fixtures should be taken into consideration and the fact should be stated. Agricultural property is to be valued in the manner prescribed by Section 7 (5), Finance Act, 1894, but it should be noted that the allowance for management expenses can only be taken if 25 years' purchase on the net annual value is given.

The deductions allowed against the principal value of the property included in the account are the incumbrances on such property which were created by deceased himself or by his predecessors in title. If created by the deceased they cannot be allowed unless incurred for full consideration in money or money's worth wholly for deceased's own use and benefit and to take effect out of his interest. If there is a right of reimbursement from any other estate or person the debt will not be allowed unless such reimbursement cannot be obtained. If the mortgage is charged on different portions of deceased's estate such debt should be apportioned. Where the debts on deceased's Real Estate exceed the value thereof a deduction of such deficiency may be taken in the schedule to the account No. 1. Any deficiency of Personal Estate shown by account No. 1 may be included in the schedule.

The account No. 5 annexed to the affidavit should not be used except for property which is chargeable with Estate Duty on deceased's death and is aggregable with deceased's own estate and then only when the duty on the property included therein is being paid upon the affidavit. If the duty on the aggregable estate is not accounted for at the time of grant, or if the property is not aggregable, a schedule should be annexed to the affidavit giving the particulars of the "other" property passing in order that in the case of aggregable property the rate of duty may be determined. For this purpose the particulars need not be in detail, but the principal value of the property must be shown as nearly as possible.

It is, however, necessary to show under what disposition the property passes and also the relationship of the beneficiaries to the deceased. Fuller particulars must be supplied when the duty is accounted for. The paragraph in the affidavit referring to such " other " property must be modified by striking out the reference to account No. 5, and the schedule above mentioned should be otherwise identified.

The rates of Estate Duty are as follows :—

Where the *net* Principal Value of the Estate				Rate per Cent.
	£		£	£ s. d.
Exceeds	100 and does not exceed		500	1
,,	500	,, ,,	1,000	2
,,	1,000	,, ,,	10,000	3
,,	10,000	,, ,,	25,000	4
,,	25,000	,, ,,	50,000	4 10 0
,,	50,000	,, ,,	75,000	5
,,	75,000	,, ,,	100,000	5 10 0
,,	100,000	,, ,,	150,000	6
,,	150,000	,, ,,	250,000	6 10 0
,,	250,000	,, ,,	500,000	7
,,	500,000	,, ,,	1,000,000	7 10 0
,,	1,000,000	- -	- -	8

In the estates of persons dying *before* the 1st July, 1896, the duty is calculated on every £10 or fractional part of £10, so that an estate of the value of £905 is charged as £910. In cases where the fractions of the net value of the real and personal estate upon which duty is offered make together less than £10, for example £905 and £904= £1,809, the duty on the fraction is thrown upon the larger sum (in this instance on the £905), and the duty would be charged on £910 and £900 respectively. This rule would not apply if only part of the aggregated sum is being paid on the affidavit, for in this case the duty on the whole fraction would be charged.

By Section 17 of the Finance Act, 1896, it is enacted that in the estates of persons dying on or after 1st July, 1896, where the principal value of an estate comprises a fraction of £100 in excess of £100, or of any multiple of £100, such fraction is to be EXCLUDED from the value of the estate for the purpose of determining both the *rate* and the *amount* of duty; except that where the value exceeds £100 and does not exceed £200 the duty is to be £1.

For example, an estate of £10,080 is charged as an estate of £10,000, and the rate of duty being £3 per cent., the duty would be £300. An estate of £10,100 would, however, be dealt with as of that value, and the rate being £4 per cent., the duty would be £404. An estate of £594 would be charged as £500 at the rate of £1 per cent., the duty being £5.

In cases where duty is paid upon Real and Personal Estate on the affidavit for Inland Revenue on taking the grant, and there is a fraction of £100 in the value of each estate, the rule is as follows :—(1) If the two fractions together do not exceed £100, each fraction is to be left out of account; (2) if, however, the two fractions together exceed £100, the amount which has the larger fraction is to be increased to the next multiple of £100, and the other fraction is not to be considered. Thus, (1) Real Estate £740 and Personal Estate £442, total £1,182, duty is charged on £1,100, that is, £700 Real and £400 Personal; (2) Real Estate £860, Personal Estate £450, total £1,310, duty is charged on £1,300, that is, Real £900 and Personal £400.

If Estate Duty on the Real Estate is not paid on the affidavit for grant and the value of the Personal Estate is under £100 the duty is charged on the actual value of such Personal Estate.

If the duty on the Real Estate is not being paid upon the affidavit for grant the *rate* of duty is ascertained by excluding the fraction on the aggregated estate, but the amount of duty is determined by disregarding the fraction in each case except when the value of the estate upon which duty is being paid is under £100. Thus, Personal Estate £268, Real

Estate £1,478, total £1,746, the rate of duty is 3 per cent., and the duty on the Personal Estate is charged on £200. But if the Personal Estate is £70 and the Real Estate is £1,478, the rate of duty is 3 per cent., and the duty on the Personal Estate would be £2 2s. 0d., being 3 per cent. on the actual amount as explained above.

Where the *gross* value of the property, real and personal, settled and not settled, in respect of which Estate Duty is payable on the death of the deceased (exclusive of property settled otherwise than by the will of the deceased) does not exceed £300, a fixed duty of 30s., and where the gross value of such property does not exceed £500, a fixed duty of 50s. *may* be paid, instead of the *ad valorem* duty according to the scale. The court fee in each case is 15s. only.

Interest at 3 per cent. on the duty on the Personal Estate is charged from the date of death to the date of payment.

In cases where the fixed duty of 30s. or 50s. is paid within one year of the death, interest on the duty is not charged, but if the application for the grant is made after the expiration of one year from the death, interest at the rate of 3 per cent. is charged from the date of death to the date of payment. This interest is paid by means of postage stamps.

Interest on the duty on Real Estate is not chargeable until the expiration of twelve months from the date of death, except in cases where the Real Estate has been sold within that period in which case interest on the duty at 3 per cent. is charged from the date of *completion* of sale to date of payment.

Fuller particulars as to the charge of duty under the Finance Act, 1894, and the important subject of aggregation will be found in the "Handbook to the Estate Duty," by A. W. Soward, of the Legacy Duty Office, published by Waterlow and Sons Limited; who have also prepared forms for use with the various Inland Revenue affidavits, specimens of which will be forwarded on application.

DUTY-PAID STAMP OR CERTIFICATE OF PAYMENT ON AFFIDAVIT.

The Commissioners of Inland Revenue will, on presentation of a memorial, accompanied by the affidavit of value to be lodged on applying for a grant *de bonis non* or cessate grant or double probate, impress a duty-paid stamp or endorse a certificate of payment of duty on such affidavit, if duty has been paid on the original estate. If any portion of the estate to be included in the second or subsequent grant has not borne Probate or Estate Duty a corrective affidavit must be rendered and the duty paid, after which the free stamp or certificate will be impressed or endorsed.

If the deceased died *on or before* the 1st day of August, 1894, form " A " is the appropriate affidavit, but if the death was *after* the 1st of August, 1894, form " A-5 " must in every case without exception be used.

The form of memorial is as follows :—

TO THE HONOURABLE

The Commissioners of Inland Revenue.

THE MEMORIAL of [*the Memorial may be signed by the solicitor ; it must not be sent by post but presented personally, or through an agent, at the Head Office in London*]

Reg.   18   Fo.   Afft. No.

SHEWETH THAT   late of
Deceased died on the   day of   18

THAT on the   day of   18   Probate of his Will (*or as the case may be*) was granted by the   Registry of the Probate Division of the High Court of Justice to

THAT [*state here the circumstances which render the further grant necessary. The exact date of death of an Executor or Administrator should be stated.*]

THE said   swore the Personal Estate and Effects of the said Deceased to be of *or* under the value of £   and paid a Stamp Duty of £
(1) upon such grant of   which is herewith produced for inspection ; (*or*),
(2) upon the Affidavit of value for Inland Revenue which is now filed at the Legacy and Succession Duty Office). [*Strike out the words at 1 or 2 as the case may be.*]

THE Personal Estate and Effects of the said Deceased for or in respect of which the said Probate (*or as the case may be*) was granted, consisted of the items set forth in the following Account No. 1.

ACCOUNT No. 1.

THAT the Estate remaining to be administered, consists of the items set forth in the following Account No. 2.

ACCOUNT No. 2.

THE said who is [*state how entitled to new grant*] of the said now applies for a Grant of and hath sworn the Personal Estate and Effects of the said deceased to be of the value of £

YOUR MEMORIALIST therefore humbly pray that your Honourable Board will be pleased to grant the usual Duty-paid Stamp *or* Certificate of payment of Duty on the Inland Revenue Affidavit for the proposed new Grant.

DATED this day of 18
(*Signature*)

In the Account No. 1 should be inserted particulars of the assets in respect of which the original grant was obtained and their value at that date. Full description of leaseholds, stocks and shares should also be given. If the details cannot be supplied a statement to this effect must be made in the Account. The Account No. 2 should contain particulars *of the estate remaining to be administered* at the date of the memorial and the items should be identified with the assets in Account No. 1.

If the assets remaining to be administered are under the value of £100 and the deceased died on or before the 1st day of August, 1894, a free mark on the affidavit is not necessary, but if the death is after that date a memorial must in all cases be submitted in order that a certificate may be endorsed on the affidavit.

It is not necessary to produce the original grant if taken on or after the 1st day of June, 1881.

The memorial may be signed by the solicitor extracting the grant. It must not be sent by post, but must be presented personally at the Legacy Duty Office in London.

ENGROSSMENT OF WILL.

The will must be fairly and legibly engrossed on parchment, the spelling and abbreviations appearing as in the original; but the alterations (if any), if shown to have been made before execution of the will, and they are such as can be read with the will as it stood before alteration, must be written fairly as part of the text, and not fac-simile. If figures are given in the will they must appear in the engrossment. Objection is taken in the Registry to any material part of the will being written upon an erasure. When bookway skins or small open skins are used the fold must allow for the seal which is $4'' \times 4''$. The writing should be on both sides of bookway skins. The engrossment will be collated with the original will in the Registry. The folios (90 words) must be marked thereon before lodging.

Marking Exhibits.—Where only the ordinary oath is filed with the will, it is sufficient that the executors and commissioner sign the will (as also the codicil, if any) in this form—

A. B. ⎫
C. D. ⎬ *Executors,*   *E. F., Commissioner.*

no exhibit clause being required; but where any additional affidavit is to be filed, the following form should be written on the will—" This is the testamentary paper writing, or will (or codicil) referred to in the annexed affidavit of sworn on the   day of   18   before me,

E. F., Commissioner."

This latter direction does not apply to the Principal Registry and is not obligatory in some District Registries.

CHAPTER 4.

PROCEDURE.

THE papers to lead application for the grant of probate being now presumed to be in order, the practitioner will attend at the Registry with the papers as under :—

    1. Original will (and codicils if any),

    2. Oath for executors,

    3. Affidavit for Inland Revenue, duly stamped,

    4. Engrossment,

and any other affidavits necessary in proof of due execution of the testamentary papers and of their condition when executed, identity of executors, etc.; and instrument of renunciation under the hands of the renouncing executors, if any, and will make application for the fee-sheet, the form of which is given on the following page, with explanation of each item.

It may not be out of place here to suggest the desirability of papers to lead grants of probate or administration being brought into the Registry as early in the day as possible, so as to allow the officials sufficient time for careful examination, and to make the requisite searches, which latter are, in some cases, very lengthy.

In the High Court of Justice.

PROBATE, DIVORCE AND ADMIRALTY DIVISION.
(PROBATE.)

THE   REGISTRY

Deceased.

18   .

LIST OF REGISTRY FEES RECEIVED ON GRANT.

Column for affixing Fee Stamp. (a)		£	s.	d.
	1. Administering Oaths ...			
	Each Oath 1 6			
	2. Marking Exhibits ...			
	Whether on the same paper or not, 1 - each			
	3. Attesting Bond			
	1 6. Each subsequent Attestation, 1/-			
	4. Receipt	1		
	5. Notice of Application to Principal Registry	1		
	6. Filing ditto			6
	7. Certificates from Principal Registry	1		
	8. Filing ditto			6
	9. Registrar's Certificate, 2 6 ...	2		6
	Filing each Affidavit, with or without exhibits, 2 -;			
	Every other Instrument, 2 6 each			
Note.—Items 5, 6, 7, 8, 11, 16, 17, 18, 20, are not payable when the application for Grant is made in the Principal Registry.	10.			
	11. Engrossing and Collating Will for further Grant, folios			
	12. Registering and Collating Will, folios			
	13. Ditto facsimile or Pencil Marks, folios			
	14. Probate or Administration with Will under Seal. Under £ ...			
	15. Administration under Seal. Under £			
	16. Copy Will for Principal Registry, folios			
	17. Ditto facsimile or Pencil Marks, folios			
	18. Record of Grant for ditto			
	19. Search (1s)			
	20. Do. in Principal Registry			
	21. Special or Limited Grant, folios			
	22. Settling draft Oath to lead ditto			
	23. Enrolment of ditto, folios ..			
	24. Ditto Bond, folios			
	Where the Property to be dealt with is under £20, 1/- per folio : above £20 2 - per folio.			
	25. Collating Documents and Certificate ..			
	26. Fiat...			
	27. Noting Record of First Grant ...	2		6
	28. Noting Domicile			
	£	.		

(a) The Stamps to be used are "Judicature Fee Stamps," and so marked, they are of the values of 1d., 2d., 6d., 1.-, 1.6, 2.-, 2.6, 3/-, 5.-, 10.-, £1, £2, £5.

Nos. 1, 2 and 3. These charges are made when papers are sworn to in the Registry.

4. When the papers are handed into the Registry, the practitioner will receive from an officer of the Court a temporary voucher for them, which voucher should be returned to the Registry when the grant is received. This fee of 1s. is charged for preparing the voucher.

5. This notice to lead certificate from Principal Registry is prepared in the Registry, and the fee of 1s. charged for preparing it.

6. When the certificate has been received from the Principal Registry, it is filed with the papers, and the fee of 6d. charged for filing it.

7. This fee is for the certificate issued from the Principal Registry when the application is made through a District Registry.

8. This is the fee 6d. for filing the above in the Registry.

9. This fee is charged for the certificate by the Registrar at the foot of the grant as to the gross value of the personal estate (required by Act of Parliament).

10. Here should be inserted all affidavits and other documents which are to be filed in the Registry. No charge is made for filing oath or bond, or affidavit for Inland Revenue.

11. Where a grant of double probate or administration with the will *de bonis non* is applied for in the District Registry, the engrossment is made in the Registry, and a fee of 4s. 6d. for the first three folios, and 1s. 6d. for every additional folio is charged. (Extra words over the folio being in all cases counted as a folio.)

12. This fee is also at the rate of 4s. 6d. for the first three folios, and 1s. 6d. for every additional folio.

13. This fee is at the rate of 1s. for the first two folios, and 6d. for every additional folio, and is charged in addition to the fees in No. 12.

14. Here is inserted the fee charged upon the *net* amount of estate according to the scale. (*See* p. 118.)

15. The same herein.

16. The charge of 2s. 6d. for the first five folios, and 6d. for every additional folio, is made for this copy, which is sent to the Principal Registry with the weekly return.

17. *See* No. 13.

18. This fee is charged for the record of the grant filed in the Registry, a duplicate of which is sent to London with the weekly return. Where the record exceeds five folios in length, in case of a limited or special grant, it is charged at the rate of 6d. per folio.

19. The fee of 6d. for every full year or part of year is charged for making search in the Registry, the calculation being made from the date of death to application for the grant.

20. The fee of 6d. a year is charged for making this search in the Principal Registry where the calendars are not complete in the District Registry.

21. This fee is charged at 1s. per folio where the estate to be placed in the possession of or dealt with by the administrator by means of the grant is under £20, but at 2s. a folio when it exceeds that sum.

22. This fee is 2s. 6d. for 10 folios and under, and 3d. for every additional folio.

23. The same as 21.

24. In cases of special grants the bond is prepared in the Registry, and the same fee as in No. 21 is charged.

25. This fee is 2s. 6d. for 10 folios and under, and 3d. for every additional folio.

26. *See* Registrar's Fiat, referred to in Chapter 1, page 115. The practitioner makes the copy will according to the particular circumstances of the case.

27. This fee is charged in case of a second or supplementary grant.

28. This fee relates to cases in which Scotch property is included in the Affidavit for Inland Revenue and to which reference is made in the Oath. (*See* page 101.)

CHAPTER 5.

ADMINISTRATION WITH THE WILL ANNEXED.

WHEN the practitioner receives a will for the purpose of proving the same, and there are no executors thereby appointed; or if any appointed, they have died before the testator, or, having survived him, have died without having proved the will; or have renounced probate ; or being resident abroad, have appointed an attorney to act for them, the Court will grant administration (with the will annexed) of the Personal Estate and effects of the deceased.

The renunciation by an executor of probate of the will includes a renunciation of his right to administration with the will annexed if he is entitled to such grant as residuary legatee in trust or otherwise.

The same rules as to the execution of the will, etc., referred to in Chapter 1, are equally applicable to a will annexed to a grant of administration.

The grant is made to the persons interested in the following order :—

1. Attorney of executor (who resides out of England).

2. Universal (or residuary) legatees in trust (one or more of them, not exceeding three).

3. Residuary legatees for life (one or more).

4. Residuary legatees substituted on the decease of those who take a life interest (one or more).

5. Residuary legatees (one or more).

6. The legal personal representatives of residuary legatees who survived the testator, but have since died, in cases where *all* the residuary legatees are dead. The grant constituting such legal personal representative or, if same not available, a copy of the Act of Probate or Administration must be produced. The Court always prefers a living person, entitled in distribution, to the representative of a deceased residuary legatee.

7. The next-of-kin when no residuary legatee is appointed or when the gift of residue has lapsed.

8. A legatee.

A few examples of the foregoing forms of grant will be found in the next chapter.

Where there is any doubt as to the interest of the applicant in respect of which a grant should be made, the opinion of the Registrar should first be taken in order to avoid error.

In addition to the ordinary oath (described in the next chapter), and affidavit for Inland Revenue, the Court requires a bond to be given by the administrator (will). (*See* Chapter 7.)

For the Inland Revenue affidavit and special instructions thereon, see Chapter 3.

A certificate of the practitioner as to the cause of delay in applying for a grant is required when the application is not made until three years after testator's death. (*See* Certificate of delay, p. 132.)

Seven clear days must elapse from the death of testator before a grant of administration (will) can be made to his estate.

CHAPTER 6.

OATH FOR ADMINISTRATORS (WITH THE WILL ANNEXED).

RULE 43 directs that, "the oath of administrators, and of administrators with the will annexed, is to be so worded as to clear off all persons having a prior right to the grant, and the grant is to show on the face of it how the prior interests have been cleared off and the oath is to set forth, when the fact is so, that the party applying is the only next-of-kin of the deceased."

The form of oath is given here at full length, in order to explain the blanks numerically.

[*Oath—For Administrators with the Will.*]

In the High Court of Justice.

PROBATE, DIVORCE AND ADMIRALTY DIVISION.
(PROBATE.)

THE   REGISTRY

IN the goods of   deceased
(¹) I,   of   make oath and say that,   believe the paper writing   hereto
annexed, and marked by   to contain the true and original last will and
testament (²)   of (³)
of (⁴)   deceased, who died (⁵) on the   day of   18   , at
and that (⁶)   and
that   will faithfully administer the personal estate and effects of the said
                        deceased by paying h   just debts, and the legacies contained in
h   Will   and distributing the residue of h   estate according to
law ; that   will exhibit a true and perfect inventory of all and singular the said
personal estate and effects, and render a just and true account thereof whenever
required by law so to do; and that the gross personal estate and effects of the said
deceased is of the value of £*   and no more to the best of
knowledge, information, and belief.

Sworn at
on the   ⎫
                                            18   ,⎭
        Before me,
                                    A Commissioner for Oaths.

* As to the amount to be inserted here, *see* page 17.

1. *See* 1, Chapter 2.

2, 3, and 4. *See* 2, 3, 4, 5, Chapter 2.

6. Here all persons having a prior right to the grant in the order set forth on pages 46 and 47 should be cleared off.

The interest in respect of which the applicant proposes to take the grant should then be shown.

In order more perfectly to illustrate these two latter points, a few descriptive cases are given.

Where the applicant is related to the deceased, the relationship must be shown at No. 6. The relationship to the deceased of any persons who were entitled to the grant and are dead or have renounced must also be given. (*See* page 15.)

Where a grant of administration (will) is made to a representative of a person entitled, care must be taken that the date of the grant to the representative, and the Registry from which it issued, are correctly stated in the oath. The leading grant must be produced.

The administrator must be sworn to the oath, and must execute the bond, before the same commissioner.

EXAMPLES OF CLEARING OFF.

No executor appointed—Grant to the sister, the residuary legatee in trust.

> (6) The said deceased did not in his said will name any executor; that I am the sister of the said deceased, and the residuary legatee in trust named in his said will.

No executor appointed—Grant to child one of the residuary legatees.

> (6) The said deceased did not in his said will name any executor; that I am the son of the said

E

deceased and one of the residuary legatees named in his said will.

[NOTE.—It sometimes happens that a testator bequeaths his estate to a person subject to a condition, *e.g.*, on condition that the legatee does not marry outside a particular faith, in such case it must be shown that at the time of making the application for Grant the condition is complied with.]

No executor or residuary legatee—Grant to widow.

(6) The said deceased did not in his said will name any executor or residuary legatee; that I am the lawful widow and relict of the said deceased.

Executors renounce—No residuary legatee named—Grant to lawful widow and relict.

(6) *A. B.*, and *C. D.*, the executors named in the said will, have renounced the probate and execution thereof; that the said testator did not in his said will name any residuary legatee; that I am the lawful widow and relict of the said testator.

No executor or residuary legatee—Grant to brother.

(6) The said deceased did not in his said will name any executor or residuary legatee; that the said deceased died a widower without child or parent; that I am the natural and lawful brother and one of the next-of-kin of the said deceased.

Sole executor and residuary legatee survives testator and dies without proving—Grant to representative of residuary legatee.

(6) That *A. B.*, the sole executor and residuary legatee named in the said will, survived the said deceased and is since dead without having taken upon himself probate and execution thereof; that I am the executor

of the will of the said *A. B.*, deceased, I having duly proved his said will in this Division at the Principal Registry thereof on the   day of   , 18

Executors die in testator's lifetime—Grant to residuary legatee.

(6) *A. B.*, the brother of the said testator, and *C. D.*, the executors named in the said will, died in testator's lifetime; that I am the residuary legatee named in the said will.

Executors and residuary legatees in trust die in testator's lifetime—Grant to the relict of deceased the residuary legatee for life.

(6) *A. B.* and *C. D.*, the executors and residuary legatees in trust named in the said will, died in testator's lifetime ; that I am the relict of the said testator, and the residuary legatee for life named in his said will.

Executor and residuary legatee in trust, and the widow, the residuary legatee for life, both renounce —Grant to the son, one of the residuary legatees substituted.

(6) *A. B.*, the sole executor and residuary legatee in trust named in the said will, has renounced the probate and execution thereof ; that *C. D.*, widow, the relict of the said testator, the residuary legatee for life named in his said will, has renounced the letters of administration (with the said will annexed) of his personal estate ; that I am the son of the said testator, and one of the residuary legatees substituted in his said will.

One executor renounces—the other executor died in testator's lifetime—Grant to residuary legatee.

(6) *A. B.*, one of the executors named in the said will, has renounced the probate and execution thereof ; that *C. D.*, the other executor named in the said will, died in testator's lifetime ; that I am the residuary legatee named in the said will.

Executor dies in testator's lifetime—Gift of residue lapsed— Grant to brother as one of the next-of-kin.

(6) *A. B.*, the nephew and the sole executor named in the said will, died in the lifetime of testator; that *C. D.*, the son, the sole residuary legatee named in the said will, also died in the lifetime of the said testator a bachelor; that the said deceased died a widower without child or parent, that I am the natural and lawful brother and one of the next-of-kin of the said deceased.

Executor dies in testator's lifetime—Residuary legatee (the son) also dies in testator's lifetime but leaves issue— Grant to representative of dead residuary legatee [Wills Act, 1837].

(6) *A. B.*, the sole executor named in the said will, died in the lifetime of testator; that *C. D.*, the son, the sole residuary legatee named in the said will, also died in the lifetime of the said testator leaving lawful issue; that I am the executor of the will of the said *C. D.*, deceased, I having duly proved his said will in this Division at the   Registry thereof on the
day of   18

Sole executrix and residuary legatee for life dies in testator's lifetime—Residuary legatee for life substituted renounces—Grant to residuary legatee substituted.

(6) That *A. B.*, the lawful wife of the said deceased and the sole executrix and residuary legatee for life named in his said will, died in the lifetime of the said deceased ; that *C. D.*, spinster, the lawful daughter and the residuary legatee for life substituted in the said will, has duly renounced the letters of administration (with the said will annexed) of the personal estate of the said deceased ; that I am the natural and lawful son and as such one of the residuary legatees substituted in the said will.

Sole executrix and universal legatee (the widow) renounces—Grant to son one of the next-of-kin.

(6) That *A. B.*, the lawful widow and relict and the sole executrix and the universal legatee named in the said will of the said deceased, has duly renounced the probate and execution thereof and also the letters of administration (with the said will annexed) of the personal estate of the said deceased; that I am the natural and lawful son and one of the next-of-kin of the said deceased.

No executor or residuary legatee in trust appointed— Residuary legatee renounces—Grant to next-of-kin.

(6) That the said deceased did not in his said will name any executor or residuary legatee in trust ; that *A. B.*, spinster, the daughter, and the sole residuary legatee named in the said will, has duly renounced letters of administration (with the said will

annexed) of the personal estate of the said deceased;
that the said deceased died a widower; that I am the
natural and lawful son and one of the next-of-kin of
the said deceased.

*Executors and universal legatees in trust and re-
siduary legatee all survived but died without proving—
Grant to representative of residuary legatee.*

(6) *A. B.* and *C. D.*, the executors and universal
legatees in trust named in the said will, survived the
said testator, but died without taking upon themselves
the probate and execution thereof. That *E. F.*, the
residuary legatee named in the said will, also survived
the said testator, but died without taking upon himself letters of administration (with the said will
annexed) of the personal estate of the said testator;
That I am the executor [or *acting executor*] of the
will [*or the administrator of the personal estate*] of the
said *E. F.*, deceased, by virtue of a probate [or *of
letters of administration*] granted to me by this Division
at the Principal Registry thereof, on the
day of   18   .

*Two executors appointed, both survived but one died
without proving, the other renounces—Grant to widow
residuary legatee for life.*

(6) That *A. B.*, one of the executors named in the
said will, survived the said deceased and is since dead
without having taken upon himself probate and execution of the said will; that *C. D.*, the son, the other
executor named in the said will, has duly renounced
probate and execution thereof; that I am the lawful
widow and the residuary legatee for life named in the
said will.

Executors renounce—Residue bequeathed to children as a class, and not by name—Grant to son, one of the residuary legatees (a minor at the date of the will).

(6) *A. B.* and *C. D.*, the executors named in the said will, have duly renounced the probate and execution thereof; that I am the natural and lawful son of the said deceased, and as such (having attained the age of 21 years), one of the residuary legatees named in his said will.

Two executors according to the tenor both survive and die without proving; residuary legatee for life (the widow) died in lifetime of testator—Grant to son (not named) one of the residuary legatees substituted.

• (6) That *A. B.* and *C. D.*, the executors according to the tenor of the said will, survived the said deceased and are both since dead, without having taken upon themselves probate and execution of the said will; that *K. M.*, the lawful widow and the residuary legatee for life named in the said will, died in the lifetime of the said deceased; that I am the lawful son of the said deceased, and as such one of the residuary legatees substituted in the said will.

Sole executor and residuary legatee dies in testator's lifetime—Testator died a bachelor—Grant to a legatee on renunciation of father.

(6) *A. B.*, the sole executor and residuary legatee named in the said will, died in testator's lifetime; that the said testator died a bachelor; that *C. D.*, the natural and lawful father and next-of-kin of the said testator, has renounced the letters of administration

(with the said will annexed) of the personal estate of
the said testator; that I am a legatee named in the
said will.

*Sole executor and residuary legatee renounces—
Deceased dies a bachelor without parent—Grant to
next-of-kin.*

(6) *A. B.*, the sole executor and residuary legatee
named in the said will, has renounced the probate and
execution thereof ; that the said deceased died a
bachelor without parent; that I am the natural and
lawful sister, and one of the next-of-kin of the said
deceased.

*Sole executor survives but did not prove—No residuary
legatee—Grant to nephew one of the persons entitled in
distribution.*

(6) *A. B.*, the sole executor named in the said will,
survived the said deceased, and is since dead without
having taken upon himself probate and execution of the
said will ; that the said deceased did not in his said will
name any residuary legatee ; that the said deceased died
a bachelor without parent leaving *G. H.*, his natural and
lawful brother and only next-of-kin, who has duly
renounced [*or* who is since dead without having taken
upon himself] letters of administration (with the said
will annexed) of the personal estate of the said deceased ;
that I am the lawful nephew, and one of the persons
entitled in distribution to the personal estate of the said
testator, being the natural and lawful son of *H. H.*, the
natural and lawful brother also of the said testator, who
died in his lifetime, to wit on the   day of   18 .

Wife (one of the executors and the residuary legatee for life) dies in testator's lifetime—The other executor survives testator and dies without proving—Residuary legatees (minors) renounce through their guardian— Grant to a creditor. (a)

(6) The said deceased by his said will appointed his wife, *A. B.* (who died in his lifetime), and *C. D.*, executors, and his said wife residuary legatee for life. That the said *C. D.* survived the said testator, but died without having proved the said will. That *E. F.* (b) and *G. H.*, the natural and lawful and only children of the said testator, and as such the residuary legatees substituted in the said will, are now in their minority, to wit, the said *E. F.*, a minor, of the age of

years only, and the said *G. H.*, a minor, of the age of

years only. That *I. J.*, widow, the lawful aunt, and one of the next-of-kin, and the curatrix or guardian lawfully elected of the said minors, has on their part and behalf duly renounced the letters of administration with the said will annexed of the personal estate of the said testator; that I am a creditor of the said deceased.

Executor cited to accept or refuse probate does not appear—Grant to the son, one of the residuary legatees.

(6) *A. B.*, the son of the said deceased, the sole executor named in the said will, has been cited to accept or refuse probate of the said will, but has in no wise appeared, and that by an order made in this matter on the   day of   18

(a) In this case a special form of bond is required.

(b) A female minor will be described as a " spinster."

it was ordered that letters of administration, with the said will annexed, of the personal estate of the said deceased be granted to me, this deponent ; that I am the son of the said testator, and one of the residuary legatees named in his said will.

[In this case a copy of the Registrar's order will be filed, and in case there has been no personal service of the citation, the sureties will have to justify. *See* Affidavit of Justification of Sureties, p. 130].

Executors survive deceased and renounce—Grant to guardian of sole residuary legatee.

In the High Court of Justice.

PROBATE, DIVORCE AND ADMIRALTY DIVISION.

(PROBATE.)

THE   REGISTRY.

     IN the goods of   deceased.

I,   of   make oath and say that
of   deceased died at   on the   day of
                   18   having made and duly executed his last will and testament
bearing date the   day of   18   and thereof appointed
and   executors who have duly renounced probate and execution
thereof ; that   spinster the lawful daughter and the sole
residuary legatee named in the said will is now in her minority to wit of the age of
      years and upwards and under the age of 21 years ; that there is no testamentary
or other lawfully appointed guardian of the said minor ; that I am the lawful
and only [*or one of the*] next-of-kin of the said   and that she has by
an instrument in writing under her hand bearing date the   day of
18   elected or chosen me to be her curator or guardian for the purpose of taking
letters of administration (with the said will annexed) of all and singular the personal
estate and effects of the said deceased for her use and benefit and until she shall attain
the age of 21 years ; that I believe the paper writing hereto annexed and marked by
me to contain the true and original last will and testament of the said deceased ; that
I will faithfully administer the personal estate of the said deceased for the use and
benefit of the said   until she shall attain the age of 21
years by paying the just debts of the said deceased and the legacies contained in his
said will and distributing the residue of his said estate according to law ; that I will
exhibit a true and perfect inventory of all and singular the said personal estate and
effects and render a just and true account thereof whenever required by law so to do ;
and that the gross personal estate and effects of the said deceased is of the value of
£   and no more to the best of my knowledge, information
and belief.

     Sworn at

     this   day of   18 ,
     Before me

Sole executor and residuary legatee a minor Grant to guardian.

I, of make oath and say that

of deceased died on the day of 18 at having made and duly executed his last will and testament bearing date the day of 18 and thereof appointed his son sole executor and sole residuary legatee ; that the said is now in his minority to wit the age of years and upwards but under the age of 21 years ; that there is no testamentary or other lawfully appointed guardian of the said minor ; that I am the lawful and only next-of-kin of the said minor ; that the said minor has by an instrument in writing, etc., etc. [*complete as preceding form*].

In all cases of grants to guardians for the benefit of minors the proposed administrator must file a declaration of the personal estate of the deceased except where the whole estate is under the gross value of £20 or where the guardians are appointed by the High Court of Chancery or other competent Court or are the testamentary guardians of the minors. (*See* rules on pages 150 and 151. For the form of election and declaration, *see* pages 133 and 135.)

The minors must elect their next-of-kin, but if such next-of-kin renounce his right to guardianship the minors may elect their next friend. If the minors have not any blood relation an application must be made to the Queen's Proctor as to whether he will interfere on behalf of the Crown, and his decision in writing must be produced to the Registrar. If the testamentary guardian of a minor apply for grant the probate of the will of the person appointing such guardian must be produced. Administration will be granted to one of two or more testamentary guardians on consent of the other or others.

Executor resides abroad—Grant to his lawfully appointed attorney. [For Power of Attorney, *see* p. 136.]

[In this case, as the form somewhat differs from the ordinary form of oath for administrators (will), a full form is here given] :

In the High Court of Justice.

PROBATE, DIVORCE AND ADMIRALTY DIVISION.
(PROBATE.)

THE   REGISTRY.

IN the goods of   ———   deceased.

I,   of   (trade), make oath and say that of   deceased, died on the day of   18   , at   , having made and duly executed his last will and testament bearing date the   day of 18   , and thereof appointed *his son*   sole executor, who now resides at (*here insert address of executor, followed by trade*). And I further make oath and say that I am the lawfully appointed attorney of the said   as in and by a letter or power of attorney under the hand and seal of the said will more fully appear. And I further make oath and say that I believe the paper writing hereto annexed and marked by me to contain the true and original last will and testament of the said deceased, and that I will well and faithfully administer the personal estate of the said testator for the use and benefit of the said and until he shall duly apply for and obtain probate of the said will to be granted to him by paying the just debts of the said deceased, and the legacies contained in his will, and distributing the residue of his estate according to law. That I will exhibit a true and perfect inventory of all and singular the said personal estate and effects, and render a just and true account thereof whenever required by law so to do, and that the gross personal estate and effects of the said testator is of the value of (*exact gross amount*) and no more, to the best of my knowledge, information and belief.

Sworn, &c.

The power of attorney and a copy of the account No. 1 annexed to the affidavit for Inland Revenue must be filed in all cases of applications by an attorney. The power is exempt from Stamp Duty.

The court will not grant administration to the attorney of an executor to whom power has been reserved if, at the date of the application, the executor who proved is still alive.

Grant will not be given to the attorney of one of two or more executors if the others reside in the United Kingdom, unless such others renounce.

AFFIDAVIT FOR INLAND REVENUE.
See Chap. 3.

CHAPTER 7.

ADMINISTRATION (WILL) BOND.

In cases where a grant of administration (will) is made, the Court requires the administrator to enter into a bond for his faithful administration of the estate, as in the case of an ordinary intestacy. Such bond will be given to the President, for the time being, of the Probate Division of the High Court, and particular care should be taken that the sureties to the bond are responsible persons, as under certain circumstances they may be called upon by the Court to justify. A solicitor's clerk cannot be accepted as a surety, unless the solicitor extracting the grant will certify (on the back of the bond) that such clerk is good and sufficient for the amount of the bond, and that he is not a surety in any other case.

In the Principal Registry a solicitor's clerk will not under any circumstances be accepted. This rule is, in special cases, relaxed if the clerk is a relative of the proposed administrator.

Widows or spinsters are accepted as sureties; and a married woman will also be accepted as a surety, on its being shown by her affidavit that she has sufficient separate personal estate to cover the penalty in the bond.

It is no longer necessary that the husband of an administratrix should join in her administration bond. A married woman administratrix will give bond for her faithful administration as a *feme sole*.

The husband of an administratrix may therefore become a party to her bond as a surety.

In ordinary cases two sureties are required, but when the personal estate is under the *gross* value of £50, one surety only may be taken to the administration bond; and one surety is also sufficient when the husband, or his legal personal representative, administers to the estate of his wife, without regard to the amount of such estate.

In lieu of sureties the Registrars will accept the bond of a guarantee society. The usual form of bond is required and in addition an affidavit is made by an officer of the society stating the assets and liabilities of the society.

The administrator of the estate of a foreign subject who was resident abroad may, (1) if it shall be proved by affidavit that the deceased left no debts in England, or (2) by leave of a Judge at Chambers, be allowed to give bond with foreign sureties. The affidavit should be made by the administrator and must state the fact that the deceased was a foreign subject. Under special circumstances the affidavit will be accepted if made by some other person cognizant of the facts.

In all other cases sureties residing in the United Kingdom, the Channel Islands, or the Isle of Man, shall be required, except by leave of a Judge at Chambers.

It should be noted that the Court will not discharge the original sureties to a bond, nor allow other sureties to be substituted for them.

Where the *gross* personal estate does not exceed £100, there is no stamp duty payable on the bond; but where such estate exceeds £100, a stamp duty of 5s. must be impressed on the bond.

For further information in regard to bonds, *see* Rules on pages 151 and 152.

The form of bond is given here at length, and the blanks will be explained numerically.

[*Administration (Will) Bond.*]

KNOW all men by these presents that we (1)
are jointly and severally bound unto (2)

the President of the Probate Division of the High Court of Justice, in the sum of (3)
of good and lawful money of *Great Britain*, to be paid to the said (2)

or to the President of the said Division, for the time being, for which payment well and truly to be made we bind ourselves and every of us, for the whole, our heirs, executors and administrators, firmly by these presents. Sealed with our Seals. Dated the   day of   in the Year of our Lord One thousand eight hundred and

The condition of this obligation is such, that if the above-named (4)

of   of
          deceased, and who died on the   day of   18
and the intended administrator (with the Will and   codicils [*if any*] annexed) of the
personal estate and effects of the said deceased (5)
do, when lawfully called on in that behalf, make, or cause to be made, a true and perfect inventory of the personal estate and effects of the said deceased (6)
          which have or shall come to   lands, possession, or knowledge,
and the same so made do exhibit, or cause to be exhibited, into the   Registry
attached to the Probate Division of the High Court of Justice at
whenever required by law so to do. And the same personal estate and effects (7)
          do well and truly administer
(that is to say) do pay the debts of the said deceased which   did owe at
decease and then the legacies contained in the said will annexed to the said letters
of administration so to   committed, as far as the said personal estate and
effects (8)   will thereto extend, and
the law charge   And further do make, or cause to be made,
a just and true account of   said administration when   shall be thereunto
lawfully required, and all the rest and residue of the said personal estate and effects,
shall deliver and pay unto such person or persons as shall be by law entitled thereto,
then this obligation to be void and of none effect, or else to remain in full force and
virtue.

Signed, Sealed, and Delivered by the within-named ⎫
                                                                            ⎬
          In the presence of   ⎭

                    A Commissioner for Oaths.

1. Here give names, residences, and descriptions of administrator and sureties. An administratrix must be described as "spinster" or "wife of   " or "widow" as the case may be. A female surety should be similarly described.

The description "gentleman" should be avoided as being too general. If the surety has not any trade or profession he should be described as "gentleman of independent means."

A clerk should be described as " banker's clerk," or as the case may be ; an accountant should be described as " chartered accountant," or as the case may be ; a cashier should be described as " mercantile cashier " or as the case may be.

As to solicitors' clerks as sureties, *see* page 61.

2. Here insert the full title and description of the President of the Court for the time being. The title of the present judge is " The Right Honourable Sir FRANCIS HENRY JEUNE, Knight."

3. Here insert double the *gross* amount of the personal estate as shown by the affidavit for Inland Revenue affidavit or the next highest round sum.

In cases of administration *de bonis non* the penal sum is double the amount of the unadministered assets.

4. Here should be inserted the interest of the person taking the grant as in the oath, for example :—

> " Jane Brown, widow, the relict, the residuary legatee, for life, named in the will of," etc.

> " C. D., the natural and lawful son and as such one of the residuary legatees substituted in the will of," etc.

> " C. D., the lawful uncle and the curator or guardian duly elected of A. B., a minor, the lawful son and the residuary legatee named in the will of," etc.,

or as the case may be.

The interest of the person taking the grant and the name and address and date of death of the testator are held to be material, and if these are incorrectly stated the bond cannot be received.

5. This space is left for the clearing off in cases of administration (will) *durante minore ætate* or *de bonis* grants or grant to an attorney. In the first case, the clearing off is similar to this, " for the use and benefit of the said minors *and infants*, and until one of them shall attain the age of 21 years," and in the second " left unadministered by *C. D.*, widow, deceased, whilst living the relict of the said testator, and the sole executrix named in his said will," or as the case may be, and in the last case, " for the use and benefit of the said *A. B.* and until he shall duly apply for and obtain Probate of the said will to be granted to him."

The filling up of remaining blanks will suggest themselves, but in case of *de bonis non* grants the words " so left unadministered " should follow at 6, 7 and 8.

9. *The attestation clause.*—Care should be taken, before the papers are sent into the Registry, that the names of the parties in the heading of the bond, their signatures, and their names in the attestation clause agree.

If one of the parties to the bond execute same by making his mark, the fact that the bond was explained to him should be stated (*see* page 19).

The administrator must execute the bond in the presence of the Commissioner who administers the oath to him. The sureties may, if more convenient, execute before another Commissioner. If the parties are marksmen, it should be stated that the effect of the bond was duly explained, and that the mark was made in the presence of the Commissioner.

A bond executed out of the United Kingdom should be attested by a Notary Public or a British Consular Agent.

F

Alterations in bond.—Alterations made in a bond previously to execution must be initialled by the Commissioner, but if made after the execution, the bond must be re-executed in the presence of the same or another Commissioner; but it will be sufficient if the parties acknowledge their signatures already made, and re-deliver the bond as their act and deed. A fresh attestation clause will be written in the margin—" Re-executed by all the within-named parties (the alterations against which I have placed my initials being first made) on the   day of 18 , in the presence of   ."   An alteration, duly attested, may be made in the *penalty* of a bond prior to the grant passing the seal.

Where a bond bearing the 5s. duty has been spoiled, by reason of a fresh one having to be substituted, the Registrar will mark it as a spoiled stamp, in order that the practitioner may afterwards procure an allowance for the stamp in the usual way.

CHAPTER 8.

LETTERS OF ADMINISTRATION.

WHEN the deceased has died without making a will, or having made a will it has been found to be invalid, or when probate has been refused on account of the informality of the execution of the will, a grant of letters of administration of the personal estate of the deceased will be made to the person entitled thereto, according to the Statutes of Distribution, *see* Table on page 178.

The relations of the deceased are entitled to the above grant in the following order :—

DECEASED DIES.	GRANT MADE TO (a)
Married ...	The surviving husband or wife.
A widower (or widow)	The child or one or more of the children.
A widower (or widow) without child	The grandchild or one or more of the grandchildren.
A bachelor (or spinster) ; or a widower (or widow) without child or other issue ...	The father as next-of-kin.
A bachelor (or spinster) ; or a widower (or widow) without child or father ...	The mother as only next-of-kin.

(a) See also page 76 for filling up Oath

DECEASED DIES.	GRANT MADE TO.
A bachelor (or spinster) ; or a widower (or widow) without child or parent ...	The brother or sister as next-of-kin.
A bachelor (or spinster) ; or a widower (or widow) without child or parent, brother or sister ...	The uncle or aunt, nephew or niece as next-of-kin.
A bachelor (or spinster) ; or a widower (or widow) without child or parent, brother or sister, uncle or aunt, nephew or niece ...	The cousin - german (first cousin) as next-of-kin.
A bachelor (or spinster) ; or a widower (or widow) without child or parent, brother or sister, uncle or aunt, nephew or niece, or cousin-german	The cousin - german once removed as next-of-kin.

A grant is made to the first next-of-kin of an intestate who applies for it without the necessity of the other next-of-kin renouncing. If so desired, there is no objection to two or three of the next-of-kin joining in the grant, but a grant will not be made to more than three except under special circumstances.

It must be remembered that the term " next-of-kin " of an intestate means those persons who were next-of-kin *at the death* of an intestate. (The words " next-of-kin," applied to the widow or husband, are erroneous.)

If the person or persons first entitled to a grant as next-of-kin, die without taking it, or renounce their right to it, the grant will go to one or more of the persons entitled in distribution. If all the persons so entitled are dead (having survived the deceased), the grant will go to the legal personal representatives (*i.e.*, executor or administrator) of any one of them.

The probate or letters of administration constituting such legal personal representative must be produced. If the original grant is not available a copy of the Act of Probate or Administration will be accepted.

The Court always prefers a living person entitled in distribution to the representative of a dead next-of-kin.

On the renunciation and consent of all the next-of-kin and the persons entitled in distribution to the personal estate of the deceased the grant will be given to a creditor who must give bond to pay the debts of the deceased *pro rata.* If there are no known relations of the deceased the next-of-kin must be cited before the grant will issue to the creditor.

A certificate of delay is required where application is not made until three years have elapsed since the death of intestate. (*See* p. 132.)

Fourteen clear days must elapse from the date of death before a grant of administration can issue to the estate of an intestate. In cases of great urgency this rule is waived by an order of the Registrar upon filing an affidavit, giving the reasons why the grant is required immediately. The Registrars are extremely reluctant to depart from the rule.

A bond [*see* p. 83] will be required to be given by the administrator for his due administration of the estate.

Application may be made under 16*th Section of the Finance Act*, 1894, if the effects (real and personal) do not exceed £500 without deduction of debts, and the intestate died after the 1st August, 1894. The fees are 15s.

only, with the addition of a stamp duty of 30s. if the effects (exceeding £100) are under £300, and 50s. if under £500.

The papers necessary to lead grant of administration are—the oath, the Inland Revenue affidavit and bond. The oath will be referred to and explained in the following chapter. For instructions as to filling up the Affidavit for Inland Revenue, *see* Chapter 3; and for preparing the Bond, *see* page 84.

Administration during minority. Where the next-of-kin are minors (i.e., above seven years of age), they must elect as their guardian one of their next-of-kin for the purpose of taking out a grant of administration for their use and benefit. If the next-of-kin of the minors renounce their guardianship, the minors may elect their next friend. (For form of election, *see* p. 135.)

All the minors must join in the election unless any are out of the United Kingdom, in which case the fact must be stated in the form of election. If any of the minors refuse to join in the election they must be cited.

If the minors have not any blood relation an application must be made to the Queen's Proctor as to whether he will interfere on behalf of the Crown, and his decision in writing must be produced to the Registrar.

If the testamentary guardian of a minor apply for grant, the probate of the will of the person appointing such guardian must be produced. Administration will be granted to one of two or more testamentary guardians on consent of the other or others.

Where there are both minors and infants (under seven years of age), the guardian elected by the minors may act on behalf of the infants if the object be to take a grant. If the object be to renounce a grant, the guardian must be specially assigned to the infants by order of the Judge or of a Registrar of the Principal Registry, and to obtain this order it should be shown by affidavit that there would be no advantage to the minors and infants in reserving to them the right to administer on attaining the age of 21 years.

Where the next-of-kin are infants, a guardian must be assigned (by Registrar's order) to take out administration on their behalf. Rule 34 says: "In all cases of infants (*i.e.*, under the age of seven years), a guardian must be assigned by order of the Judge or of one of the Registrars of the Principal Registry; the Registrar's order is to be founded on an affidavit (*see* page 128) showing that the proposed guardian is either *de facto* next-of-kin of the infants, or that their next-of-kin *de facto* has renounced his or her right to the guardianship, and is consenting to the assignment of the proposed guardian and that such proposed guardian is ready to undertake the guardianship." The affidavit referred to should be headed "Principal Registry," and (if application for grant is made in the District Registry) the District Registrar will transmit it to the Principal Registrars along with 4s. 6d., the fees for the order. When the District Registrar has received the order he will transmit it to the practitioner, who will then prepare the necessary papers, namely, the oath, Inland Revenue affidavit, bond (and declaration if the effects are £20 and upwards), and forward them to the Registry in the usual way. The fee of 2s. 6d. is charged for filing the Registrar's order, and 2s. 6d. for filing the declaration.

A guardian, as administrator, must file a declaration on oath of the personal estate of the intestate in all cases, except where the estate is under £20. (For form of declaration, *see* page 71).

[Oath to lead grant of administration to the guardian of minors and infants.]

In the High Court of Justice.

PROBATE, DIVORCE AND ADMIRALTY DIVISION.
(PROBATE.)

THE   REGISTRY.

IN the goods of HENRY BROWN, deceased.

I, Jane Brown, of No. 20, John Street, in the City of Durham, spinster, make oath and say, that Henry Brown, of the City of Durham, grocer, deceased, died on the day of   18   at   [having a fixed place of abode at   ] a widower, and intestate, leaving Mary Brown, spinster, John Henry Brown and Ernest Brown, his natural and lawful and only children, and only next-of-kin, who are now in their minority and infancy respectively, to wit, the said Mary Brown, being a minor, of the age of 15 years only; the said John Henry Brown, being a minor, of the age of ten years only; and the said Ernest Brown, being an infant, of the age of five years only. That there is no testamentary or other lawfully appointed guardian of the said minors and infant, that I am the lawful aunt and only [or *one of the*] next-of-kin of the said minors and infant, and that the said minors have, by an instrument in writing bearing date the 10th day of January, 1884, elected or chosen me to be their curatrix or guardian, for the purpose of taking out letters of administration of the personal estate of the said intestate, to be granted to me for the use and benefit of the said minors, and until one of them shall attain the age of 21 years; that I will faithfully administer the personal estate of the said intestate for the use and benefit of the said minors and infant, and until one of them shall attain the age of 21 years, by paying his just debts and distributing the residue of his estate according to law; that I will exhibit a true and perfect inventory of the said estate, and render a just and true account thereof whenever required by law so to do; and that the gross personal estate and effects of the said intestate is of the value of One thousand three hundred and one pounds five shillings and nine pence, and no more, to the best of my knowledge, information and belief.

Sworn, &c.

[Oath for mother of minors a Statutory Guardian— Guardianship of Infants Act, 1886.]

(USUAL HEADING.)

I   of   widow, make oath and say that of   deceased, died on the   day of   18   at intestate, a widower without child, leaving   spinster, and   his lawful grandchildren and only next-of-kin him surviving; that the said   and   are now in their minority, to wit, the said   being a minor of the age of   years only, and the said being a minor of the age of   years only; that I am the natural and lawful mother and the lawful guardian of the said   and   ; that I will faithfully administer, etc. [*and so on to the end as in preceding form*].

[*Oath for Guardian of Infant.*]

(USUAL HEADING.)

I   of   make oath and say as follows :—

1. That   of   deceased, died on the   day of
18   at   intestate, a widower, leaving   spinster, his natural
and lawful and only child, who is now in her infancy, to wit, of the age of   years
only and under the age of seven years.

2. That there is no testamentary or other lawfully appointed guardian of the said
infant.

3. That I am the lawful grandfather and only next-of-kin of the said infant and
that I have been duly assigned her curator, or guardian, for the purpose of taking
letters of administration of the personal estate of the said deceased for the use and
benefit of the said infant and until she shall attain the age of 21 years.

4. That I will faithfully administer the personal estate of the said deceased for the
use and benefit of the said infant and until she shall attain the age of 21 years, by
paying, etc., etc. [*as in preceding form to the end*].

The papers necessary are Election, Oath, Inland Revenue
Affidavit, Bond and Declaration (the latter, if the effects
amount to £20 and upwards). The fee of 2*s.* 6*d.* each
is charged for filing the Election and Declaration.

Administration to the attorney of a person entitled to
administration resident out of England will be granted,
without notice to the other next-of-kin. The power of
attorney must be filed, and such power and the notarial
certificate and declaration annexed thereto are not liable
to stamp duty. If, however, the power refers to other
matters the Deed and the papers annexed thereto must
be stamped and a copy will be accepted. The original Deed
must be produced and will be returned when the copy is
filed.

The following is the form of oath :—

In the High Court of Justice.

PROBATE, DIVORCE AND ADMIRALTY DIVISION.

(PROBATE.)

THE   REGISTRY.

IN the goods of   deceased.

I,   of   make oath and say that

of   in the   of

deceased died on the   day of   18   , at

intestate, a widower, leaving C.D., his natural and lawful and only son and only next-

of-kin, who is now residing at   in the   of   that

I am the lawful attorney of the said   and that

will faithfully administer the personal estate of the said deceased for the use

and benefit of the said

and until   he   shall duly apply for and obtain letters of

administration of the personal estate of the said deceased to be granted to   h   by

paying h   just debts, and distributing the residue of the said estate according to

law; that   will exhibit a true and perfect inventory of all and singular the said

estate and render a just and true account thereof whenever required by law so to do,

and that the gross personal estate and effects of the said deceased is of the value of

£   and no more, to the best of   knowledge, information and belief.

Sworn by the above-named

at   on the   day

of   18   .

Before me   A Commissioner for Oaths.

On an application for administration by an attorney a copy of the account No. 1 annexed to the Inland Revenue affidavit must be filed with the papers.

If the next-of-kin of an intestate is a lunatic not so found by inquisition, administration will be granted to the next-of-kin of such lunatic for his use and benefit during lunacy. The fact that the next-of-kin is a person of unsound mind must be proved by affidavit (*see* page 129). The following is the form of oath :—

(USUAL HEADING.)

I   of   make oath and say as follows :—

1. The said   of   spinster, deceased, died on the   day of

18   intestate, a spinster, leaving   her natural and lawful

father and next-of-kin, her surviving.

2. That the said   is now and has been for many years past a lunatic

or person of unsound mind.

3. That no committee has been appointed of the personal estate of the said

the lunatic aforesaid, nor has any person been entrusted with the applica-

tion thereof under the Lunacy Act, 1890.

4. That I am the lawful wife of the said   the lunatic aforesaid, and

that I will faithfully administer the personal estate of the said deceased for the use and

benefit of the said   during his lunacy, by paying her just debts, etc.

[*as in the preceding form to the end*].

The proposed administrator must file a declaration of the personal estate of the deceased (page 133), and the sureties to the bond must make an Affidavit of Justification (page 130).

CHAPTER 9.

OATH FOR ADMINISTRATORS.

In order more particularly to describe the filling-up of this form, it is given here at length, and the blanks will be referred to numerically.

[*Oath for Administrators.*]

In the High Court of Justice.

PROBATE, DIVORCE AND ADMIRALTY DIVISION.

(PROBATE.)

THE   REGISTRY.

IN the goods of   deceased,
(¹) I

make oath and say, that (²)   of   deceased died
on the   day of   18   , at   and
intestate ; (³)   and that I am (⁴)   that   will faithfully
administer the personal estate and effects of the said deceased by paying h   just
debts, and distributing the residue of h   estate and effects according to law ;
that   will exhibit a true and perfect inventory of all and singular
the said estate and effects, and render a just and true account thereof whenever
required by law so to do ; and that the gross personal estate and effects of the said
deceased is of the value of   and no more, to the best of   knowledge,
information and belief.

Sworn at
on the   day
of   18   .
Before me
A Commissioner for Oaths.

1. Here insert full Christian names and surnames of administrator, with place of abode and occupation or addition. (*See* page 12.) The relationship of the administrator to the intestate is *not* to be inserted here.

2. Here insert full Christian names and surname of intestate, with place of residence and description at the time of his death, and any former residence and description necessary to identify him.

The status of a female should be given as "widow," "spinster," *or* "wife of   ."

3 & 4. Particular attention must be paid to the filling-in of these two blanks. No. 3 is intended for the insertion of the words "a bachelor," or "spinster," "a widower," or "widow," as the case may be, and showing that no relation having a prior right survived the intestate, or in case any had survived that such relation had renounced or had since died without having taken administration.

No. 4 must show the interests in which the administrator claims to take the grant. The following description of such interests as described in grants of administration will be useful for reference :—

A husband	"The lawful husband."
A wife	"The lawful widow and relict."
A father	"The natural and lawful father and next-of-kin."
A mother ...	"The natural and lawful mother and only next-of-kin."
A child	"The natural and lawful son [or daughter] and only [or one of the] next-of-kin."
A brother or sister ...	"The natural and lawful brother [or sister]."

If there be no parents living, the brother or sister is further to be described as "one of the next-of-kin." or the "only next-of-kin."

A nephew or niece ...	"The lawful nephew," and "one of the" *or* "the only next-of-kin."

If a brother or sister be living, and the nephew or niece, being the child of a brother or sister of the intestate, who died in his lifetime, apply for administration, he or she is to be described as "one of the persons entitled in distribution to the personal estate of the deceased."

A Grandparent, Grand-
  child, cousin-german,
  etc. ...   . "The lawful   and one of the next-
                       of-kin," *or* " only next-of-kin."

In order to illustrate these points (3 & 4) more fully,
a number of examples are given as follows:—

*Wife dies in lifetime of her husband—Grant to
husband.*—Deceased died intestate; (2) to be here described as "wife of me, this deponent," (3) (here rule up
blank), and that I am (4) "the lawful husband of the said
intestate."

*Wife dies in lifetime of her husband who is
since also dead—Grant to executors of husband.*—
Deceased died intestate, (3) "leaving *A. B.*, her lawful
husband, who has since died without having taken upon
himself letters of administration of her personal estate,"
and that we are [*or* I am one of] (4) "the executors of the
will with a codicil thereto (if any) of the said *A. B.*, I
having duly proved the same in this Division at the
Registry thereof on the   day of   , 18 ."

> [NOTE.—One of two or more executors may apply, but adminis-
> trators must apply jointly. The leading Grant or Copy Act
> must be produced. If the executor of the husband renounces,
> grant will be given to the residuary legatee named in the will
> of the husband.]

Wife survives—Grant to widow—Deceased died
intestate, (3) (here rule up blank), and that I am (4) "the
lawful widow and relict of the said intestate."

> [NOTE.—The Registrar will in some cases grant administration to the
> widow and one of the next-of-kin of the deceased if it can be
> shown by affidavit that this course will be for the benefit of
> the estate. The affidavit must be made by the widow, who
> should state that she is aware of her right to grant solely. The
> names of the beneficiaries should be given in the affidavit and
> their consent to the grant must be obtained.]

Deceased dies intestate—Widow survives, but dies without taking—Grant to son.—Deceased died intestate, (3) "leaving *A. B.*, widow, his lawful widow and relict, who has since died without having taken upon herself letters of administration of his personal estate," and that I am (4) "the natural and lawful son and *only* next-of-kin of the said intestate."

On renunciation of widow — Grant to son. — Deceased died intestate, (3) "leaving *C. D.*, widow, his lawful widow and relict, who has duly renounced the letters of administration of his personal estate," and that I am (4) "the natural and lawful son, and *one of the* next-of-kin of the said intestate."

Deceased dies a widow—Grant to son.—Deceased died intestate (3) "a widow," and that I am (4) "the natural and lawful son and *only* (or "one of the") next-of-kin of the said intestate."

Deceased dies a widow [or widower] without child or parent—Grant to brother.—Deceased died intestate, (3) "a widow [or widower] without child or parent," and that I am (4) "the natural and lawful brother, and *one of the* next-of-kin of the said intestate."

Deceased dies a widow without child—Grant to grandson.—Deceased died intestate, (3) "a widow without child," and that I am (4) "the lawful grandson and *one of the* next-of-kin of the said intestate."

Deceased died a widower—Grant to child.—Deceased died intestate (3) "a widower" and that I am (4) "the natural and lawful child and one of the next-of-kin of the said deceased."

Deceased dies a widower leaving a child, who has since died—Grant to grandson (son of a deceased daughter), one of the persons entitled in distribution. — Deceased died intestate, (3) " a widower, leaving *A. B.,* spinster, his natural and lawful daughter and only next-of-kin, who has since died without having taken upon herself letters of administration of his personal estate," and that I am (4) " the lawful grandson and one of the persons entitled in distribution to the personal estate of the said intestate, being the natural and lawful son of *C. D.,* widow, the natural and lawful daughter also of the said intestate and who died in his lifetime, to wit on the
day of   , 18   ."

Deceased dies a bachelor [*or spinster*]*—Grant to father.*—Deceased died intestate, (3) " a bachelor [or spinster,"] and that I am (4) "the natural and lawful father and next-of-kin of the said intestate."

Deceased dies a widower without child [*or bachelor*] *—Grant to representative of father.*—Deceased died intestate, (3) " a widower without child [*or* a bachelor] leaving *A. B.,* his natural and lawful father and next-of-kin, who has since died without having taken upon himself letters of administration of the personal estate of the said intestate," and that I am (4) " the administrator of the personal estate of the said *A. B.,* letters of administration of his personal estate having been granted to me by this Division at the   Registry thereof on the   day of   , 18   ."

Deceased dies a bachelor [*or spinster*] *without father —Grant to mother.* — Deceased died intestate, (3) " a bachelor [or spinster] without father," and that I am (4) "the natural and lawful mother and only next-of-kin of the said intestate."

Deceased dies a bachelor or spinster — Father renounces and consents—Grant to his son or daughter. —Deceased died intestate, (3), "a bachelor leaving *A. B.*, his natural and lawful father and next-of-kin, who has duly renounced the letters of administration of his personal estate and consented to the same being granted to me," and that I am (4) "the natural and lawful son [or daughter] of the said *A. B.*"

Deceased died a spinster without father—Grant to brother on renunciation of mother. - Deceased died intestate (3) "a spinster without father leaving widow, her natural and lawful mother and only next-of-kin, who has duly renounced letters of administration of the personal estate of the said intestate," and that I am (4) "the natural and lawful brother of the said deceased."

Deceased died a bachelor without father leaving mother since also dead—Grant to brother.—Deceased died intestate (3) "a bachelor without father, leaving widow, his natural and lawful mother and only next-of-kin, who is since dead without having taken upon herself letters of administration of the personal estate and effects of the said intestate," and that I am (4) "the natural and lawful brother of the said deceased."

Deceased died a bachelor [or spinster] without parent —Grant to brother.—Deceased died intestate (3) "a bachelor [or spinster] without parent," that I am (4) "the natural and lawful brother and one of the next-of-kin of the said deceased."

Deceased dies a bachelor, without parent, brother or sister—Grant to nephew (or niece, or uncle, or aunt). —Deceased died intestate, (3) "a bachelor, without parent, brother or sister," and that I am (4) the "lawful [nephew] and *one of the* next-of-kin of the said intestate."

Deceased dies a widow, without child or parent—On renunciation of brother or sister—Grant to one of persons entitled in distribution.—Deceased died intestate, (3) "a widow without child or parent, leaving *A. B.* [widow] her natural and lawful [sister] and only next-of-kin, who has duly renounced the letters of administration of her personal estate," and that I am (4) "the lawful niece, and one of the persons entitled in distribution to the personal estate of the said intestate, being the natural and lawful daughter of *C. D.*, widow, the natural and lawful sister also of the said intestate, and who died in her lifetime, to wit on the   day of   , 18   ."

Deceased dies leaving widow and children all since deceased—Grant to administrator of one of them.—Deceased died intestate, (3) "leaving *A. B.*, his lawful widow and relict, and *C. D.* and *E. F.*, spinster, his natural and lawful children and only next-of-kin, and together the only persons entitled in distribution to his personal estate, who have all since died without having taken upon themselves letters of administration of the personal estate of the said intestate," and that I am (4) "the administrator of the personal estate of the said *A. B.* [or *C. D.*, or *E. F.*], letters of administration of the personal estate of the said having been granted to me by this Division at the Registry thereof, on the   day of   , 18   ."

Deceased dies a widower without child [or bachelor] or parent, brother or sister, uncle or aunt, nephew or niece—Grant to cousin-german.—Deceased died intestate, (3) "a widower without child or parent [or bachelor without parent], brother or sister, uncle or aunt, nephew or niece," and that I am (4) "the lawful cousin-german and one of the next-of-kin of the said intestate."

G

Deceased dies a bachelor without parent, brother or sister, uncle or aunt, nephew or niece, or cousin-german —Grant to first cousin once removed.—Deceased died intestate (3) "a bachelor without parent, brother or sister, uncle or aunt, nephew or niece, or cousin-german," and that I am (4) "the lawful first cousin once removed and only next-of-kin of the said deceased."

Deceased dies leaving husband an undischarged bankrupt—He renounces—Grant to Official Receiver in Bankruptcy.—Deceased died intestate, (3), "leaving the said *E. F.*, her lawful husband, her surviving; that the said *E. F.* has duly renounced letters of administration of her personal estate and effects; that the said *E. F.* was on the   day of   , 189   , adjudicated a bankrupt on a Receiving Order, dated the   day of   , 189   , of the County Court of   holden at   ; that no order for his discharge has yet been made, (4) and that I am the trustee of the estate of the said *E. F.*, as such Official Receiver as aforesaid."

Deceased died a widower [or bachelor] without child or parent—On renunciation of next-of-kin grant to creditor.—Deceased died intestate (3) "a widower without child or parent [or bachelor without parent] leaving   widow, his natural and lawful sister and only next-of-kin and the only person entitled in distribution to his personal estate, who has duly renounced letters of administration of his said personal estate," and that I am (4) "a creditor of the said deceased."

For instructions as to filling up of remaining blanks, *see* Chapter 2.

Affidavit for Inland Revenue, see Chapter 3.

BOND (*Intestacy.*)

K NOW All Men by these Presents, That We

are jointly and severally bound unto The Right Honourable, the President of the Probate Division of the High Court of Justice, in the Sum of Pounds, of good and lawful Money of *Great Britain*, to be paid to the said

or to the Judge of the Probate Division of the said Court for the time being, for which payment well and truly to be made we bind ourselves and of us, for the Whole, our Heirs, Executors, and Administrators, firmly by these Presents. Sealed with our Seals. Dated the day of in the Year of our Lord One Thousand Eight Hundred and

The Condition of this Obligation is such, that if the above-named the (4) of (*name*) of (*address and description*) deceased, who died on the day of 18 , and the intended Administrator of the Personal Estate and Effects of the said Deceased (5)

do, when lawfully called on in that behalf, make, or cause to be made, a true and perfect Inventory of all and singular the Personal Estate and effects of the said deceased which have or shall come to

lands, possession, or knowledge, or into the hands and possession of any other person for , and the same so made to exhibit, or cause to be exhibited, into the District Registry attached to the Probate Division of Her Majesty's High Court of Justice at , whenever required by law so to do. And the same Personal Estate and effects, and all other the Personal Estate and effects of the said deceased at the time of death, which at any time after shall come to the hands or possession of the said

or into the hands or possession of any other person or persons for , do well and truly administer according to Law (that is to say) do pay the debts to which did owe at

decease; And further do make, or cause to be made, a just and true account of said administration, whenever required by law so to do, and all the rest and residue of the said Personal Estate and effects do deliver and pay unto such Person or Persons as shall be entitled thereto, under an Act of Parliament intituled "*An Act for the better Settling of Intestate Estates.*" And if it shall hereafter appear that any last will and testament was made by the said deceased, and the executor or executors or other persons therein named do exhibit the same into the Probate Division of the said Court, making request to have it allowed and approved accordingly, if the said being thereunto required, to render and deliver the letters of administration granted (approbation of such Testament being first had and made) into the Probate Division of the said Court, then this obligation to be void and of none effect, or else to remain in full force and virtue.

Signed, sealed, and delivered
by the within named in
the presence of

A Commissioner for Oaths.

G 2

The foregoing form of bond is used in all cases of ordinary administration.

The description of the proposed administrator's interest and the name, address and description and date of death of the deceased are held to be material to the Bond.

Examples of the special wording for the blank marked (4) showing the interest of the person taking the grant are here given. It will be observed that the words follow closely the form of the oath.

> (4) " The lawful widow and relict of *A. B.*, etc."

> (4) " The natural and lawful son and one of the next-of-kin of *A. B.*, etc."

> (4) " The administrator of the personal estate of *C. B.*, deceased, the lawful husband of *A. B.*, etc."

> (4) " The natural and lawful mother and the lawful guardian of   and   minors, the lawful grandchildren and the only next-of-kin of *A. B.*, etc."

> (4) " The lawful uncle and the curator or guardian duly elected of *D. B.*, a minor, the natural and lawful son and only next-of-kin of *A. B.*, etc."

> (4) " The lawful attorney duly appointed of *C. B.*, the natural and lawful brother and only next-of-kin of *A. B.*, etc."

> (4) " The lawful wife of *F. B.*, a lunatic or person of unsound mind, the natural and lawful father and next-of-kin of *A. B.*, etc."

The blank space at (5) is for use in the case of grant to a guardian, or an attorney, or to the next-of-kin of a lunatic, or in a grant *de bonis non*.   For example :—

> *Grant to guardian.*—(5) " For the use and benefit of the said minor and until he shall attain the age of twenty-one years."

> *Grant to attorney.*—(5) " For the use and benefit of the said *C. B.*, and until he shall duly apply for and obtain letters of administration of the personal estate of the said deceased to be granted to him."

Grant to next-of-kin of a lunatic.—(5) " For the use and benefit of the said *F. B.* during his lunacy."

Grant de bonis non.—(5) " Left unadministered by *C. B.*, widow, deceased, whilst living the lawful widow and relict of the said deceased."

———

The instructions given in Chapter 7 as to the sureties, the penalty and the execution of a bond for administration (will) are applicable to a bond in an intestacy.

CHAPTER 10.

WILLS OF MARRIED WOMEN.

ON and after the 19th April, 1887, to establish a claim for a grant of probate of the Will or of Letters of Administration with Will annexed of the personal estate of a Married Woman or of a Widow whose Will was made during coverture, it will be unnecessary to recite in the oath the power in execution of which the Will has been made, or to set out the separate Personal Estate passing under the Will, or, in fact, to allege that the testatrix was possessed of any separate Personal Estate. The Grant will be made in respect of the whole personal property of the testatrix, and take the form of ordinary grants of probate and letters of administration with Will annexed, and will issue to executors or residuary legatees, as the case may be, and, in the event of a partial intestacy, to the surviving husband. As there will not in future be any limitation or specialty in the grants to be issued, there will no longer be any necessity for the settlement of draft oaths. The new rules are not applicable to cases in which any second or subsequent grant is required to complete a representation where a limited or special grant has already issued.

The ordinary oath for executors (Chapter 2) and for Administrators with the Will annexed (Chapter 6) will now be used.

CHAPTER II.

DOUBLE PROBATE.

Where power has been reserved in an original grant of probate to one or more of the executors to come in afterwards and prove, and it becomes necessary that such executors, or either of them to whom power has been reserved, should join in the administration of the estate, the Court will make a grant of Double Probate to such executors for that purpose.

The grant may in all cases be taken in the Principal Registry.

The papers required are the oath and Inland Revenue affidavit.

[Form of Oath for Double Probate.]

In the High Court of Justice.

PROBATE, DIVORCE AND ADMIRALTY DIVISION.
(PROBATE.)

THE   REGISTRY.

IN the goods of   deceased.

I   of   (trade) make oath and say as follows : –

1. That   of   (trade), deceased, died on the   day of   , 18   , at   , [having at the time of his death a fixed place of abode at   aforesaid, within the district of the county of   ], and having made and duly executed his last will and testament bearing date the   day of 18   and thereof appointed *his* (relationship if any) and *his* (relationship if any) executors.

2. That in the month of   18   the said   one of the said executors, proved the said will in this Division at the   Registry thereof, power being reserved of making the like grant to me the said the other executor, when I should apply for the same.

3. That I believe *the paper writing hereto annexed and marked by me to contain the true and original last will and testament* [or, if sworn upon the first grant, "the parchment exhibit hereunto annexed, partly written and partly printed, to contain the true last will and testament"] [or, if sworn upon an office copy, under seal, "the paper writing hereunto annexed to contain the true last will and testament"] of the said deceased; that I am one of the executors named in the said will, and that I will well and faithfully administer the personal estate of the said testator, by paying his just debts and the legacies contained in his said will, so far as the same shall thereto extend and the law bind me. That I will exhibit a true and perfect inventory of the said estate, and render a just and true account thereof whenever required by law so to do, and that the gross value of the unadministered personal estate of the said testator amounts to £   and no more, to the best of my knowledge, information and belief.

Sworn, &c.

If power has been reserved to an executor, who at the date of the first grant was shown to be a minor, the oath should state that he has attained the age of 21 years.

For Affidavits of Inland Revenue, *see* Chapter 3, and as to the free mark on the Affidavit, *see* page 38.

When the oath and affidavit are ready to be sworn to, the parties will attend at the Registry and be sworn upon the original will. If it is inconvenient for the parties to attend at the Registry for that purpose, they may be sworn upon the original grant of probate, or an office copy (under seal) of the will. Such original grant or office copy will have to be filed with the other papers in the Registry, and will not be delivered out.

The fee of 1s. is charged for looking up the original will, and 2s. 6d. for filing the grant or office copy under seal.

In the Principal Registry the engrossment must be made by the practitioner; such engrossment should not contain the Act of the first grant.

In the District Registry the engrossment is made in the Registry, and a charge of 4s. 6d. for the first three folios, and 1s. 6d. for every additional folio, is made for engrossing and collating.

The fee of 2s. 6d. is also charged for making the usual notations on the records.

No search fee is payable.

An office copy of the act of the first grant must be obtained and lodged with the papers.

The grant is in general terms, and is applicable to the whole personal estate of the testator, but the amount of the assets in the Oath and Inland Revenue affidavit, should only be that of the unadministered personal estate.

The seal fees, if no stamp duty is payable, are as follows :—

Personal estate under the value of :—

					s.	*d.*
£100	...				1	0
£200		...			3	0
£300		...	...		7	6
£450	...			...	12	0
Above £450	...	...	...	...	12	6

CHAPTER 12.

CESSATE GRANTS.

WHEN an executor has been appointed for life, or for a definite period, and his grant of probate, by reason of his death or otherwise, ceases to be operative ; or when any grant of administration, limited in duration, ceases, it becomes necessary that the estate should be represented, and the Court will make a second or supplemental (or as it is usually termed " Cessate ") grant of probate or administration to the person or persons next entitled to it.

PROBATE.

[Oath for cessate probate to a substituted executor.]

In the High Court of Justice.

PROBATE, DIVORCE AND ADMIRALTY DIVISION.
(PROBATE.)

THE   REGISTRY.

IN the goods of   deceased,
I,   of   (trade), make oath and say that
                       of   (trade), deceased, died on the
day of   18 , at   having made and duly executed
his last will and testament, bearing date the   day of   ,
18 , and thereof appointed his son   executor for life, and at his
said son's decease substituted his nephew (me the deponent) executor.

And I further make oath, that on the   day of   18 ,
the said   duly proved the said Will in this Division at the
Registry thereof, and is since dead, to wit, on the   day of
18 , whereby the said probate has ceased and expired :

And I further make oath, that I believe the parchment exhibit hereunto annexed partly written and partly printed and marked by me, to contain the said last will and testament of the said testator, of which probate was granted as aforesaid ; that I am the nephew of the said testator, and the executor substituted in his said will, and that I will well and faithfully administer the personal estate of the said testator by paying his just debts and the legacies contained in his said will so far as the same shall thereto extend and the law bind me ; that I will exhibit a true and perfect inventory of the said estate and render a just and true account thereof whenever required by law so to do; [that the said testator had at the time of his death a fixed place of abode at   aforesaid, within the district of the county of   ] and that the gross value of the whole of the unadministered personal estate of the said testator is of the value of £   and no more, to the best of my knowledge, information and belief.

     Sworn, &c.

The papers required are the oath and affidavit for Inland Revenue and office copy act of the first grant.

For affidavit for Inland Revenue, *see* Chapter 3, and for instructions as to duty paid stamp on such affidavit, *see* page 38.

THE PROCEDURE is the same as in the case of a Double Probate. (*See* Chapter 11.) The fees are also the same.

ADMINISTRATION (WILL).

When a grant of administration (with the will) has been made to a guardian for the use and benefit of a minor executor, and such grant has ceased by reason of the minor attaining 21, or the death of the guardian, the executor being still a minor, a further grant will be made to the executor, or to his newly-elected guardian as the case may be.

[*Form of Oath for Cessate Administration, Will.*]

𝕵n t𝖍e 𝕳ig𝖍 𝕮ourt of 𝕵ustice.

     PROBATE, DIVORCE AND ADMIRALTY DIVISION.
                (PROBATE.)
THE   REGISTRY.

    IN the goods of   deceased.

I,   of   (trade) make oath and say that   of   deceased, died on the   day of   18 , at   having made and duly executed his last will and testament, bearing date the   day of   18 , and by his said will appointed his son   sole executor, the said   being then a minor of the age of   years only.

     And I further make oath and say, that on the   day of   18 , administration (with the said will annexed) of the personal estate of the said testator was granted by this Division at the   Registry thereof to the lawful uncle, and one of the next-of-kin, and the curator or guardian duly elected of the said minor for his use and benefit, and until he should attain the age of 21 years.

     And I further make oath and say, that since the premises, to wit, on the   day of   18 , the said   has departed this life, whereby the said administration with the said will annexed has ceased and expired.

     And I further make oath and say that the said   is still in his minority, to wit, a minor of the age of   years only.

And I further make oath and say that I believe the paper writing hereto annexed and marked by me to contain the true [and original] last will and testament of the said testator; that I am the lawful uncle also and one of the next-of-kin of the said minor, and that he hath elected or chosen me to be his curator or guardian for the purpose of taking out letters of administration (with the said will annexed) of the personal estate of the said testator for his use and benefit, and until he shall attain the age of 21 years, and that I will well and faithfully administer the personal estate of the said testator for the use and benefit of the said minor, and until he shall attain the age of 21 years, by paying his just debts and the legacies contained in his said will, and distributing the residue of his estate according to law; that I will exhibit a true and perfect inventory of all and singular the said estate, and render a just and true account thereof whenever required by law so to do; [that the said testator had at the time of his death a fixed place of abode at   aforesaid within the district of the county of   ], and that the gross value of the whole of the unadministered personal estate of the said testator is [*exact gross amount*] and no more, to the best of my knowledge, information and belief.

Sworn, &c.

The papers required are the Oath, Inland Revenue Affidavit Bond, and Office copy act of first grant.

For Affidavit of Inland Revenue, *see* Chapter 3.

Bond, *see* Chapter 7.

For Procedure, *see* Chapter 11.

For Duty-paid Stamp on Affidavit, *see* page 38.

ADMINISTRATIONS.   (CESSATE.)

The two most usual forms of cessate grants of administration are made under the following circumstances, viz. :—

(1) Where a grant made to a guardian elected by the minor next-of-kin of an intestate ceases on the death of such guardian, such next-of-kin being then still in their minority, it becomes necessary that another grant of administration should be made to a newly elected guardian. The form given on the preceding page, drawn in conjunction with the framework of the form given below, will meet this case.

(2) Where a grant made to a guardian elected by a minor next-of-kin of an intestate, ceases by reason of the minor having attained his majority. The form of oath applicable to this case is here given.

(*Form of Oath.*)

In the High Court of Justice.

PROBATE, DIVORCE AND ADMIRALTY DIVISION.
(PROBATE.)

THE   REGISTRY.

IN the goods of   deceased.

I,   of   (trade), make oath and say that
of   (trade), deceased, died on the   day of   18 ,
at
18   , a widower and intestate; that in the month of
18   , letters of administration of the personal estate of the said intestate were granted
by this Division at the   Registry thereof, to   , the lawful   (relationship)
and one of the next-of-kin, and the curator or guardian lawfully elected of me the
deponent (then a minor), the natural and lawful and only child and only next-of-kin of
the said intestate, for my use and benefit, and until I should attain the age of 21 years.

And I further make oath, and say, that since the premises, to wit, on the
day of   , 18 , I, this deponent, have attained the age of 21 years, whereby
the said letters of administration have ceased and expired.

And I further make oath and say, that I am the natural and lawful son, and only
next-of-kin of the said intestate; that I will faithfully administer the personal estate
of the said intestate by paying his just debts, and distributing the residue of his said
estate according to law; that I will exhibit a true and perfect inventory of the said
estate, and render a just and true account thereof whenever required by law so to do;
and that the gross unadministered personal estate of the said intestate is of the value
of [*exact gross amount*], and no more, to the best of my knowledge, information and
belief.

Sworn, &c.

The papers required are Oath, Affidavit for Inland
Revenue, Bond and Office copy act of first grant.

For Affidavit for Inland Revenue, *see* Chapter 3, and as to
the duty paid stamp, *see* page 38.

Bond, *see* page 83.

The seal fees where no stamp duty has been paid are as
follows :—

If the personal estate is under the value of—

					s.	*d.*
£100					1	0
£200				...	4	6
£300	...	...	...	...	12	0
Above £300			...		12	6

CHAPTER 13.

GRANTS *DE BONIS NON.*

ADMINISTRATION (WITH THE WILL) *DE BONIS NON.*

WHERE Probate of a will has been granted to the executors named therein, and such executors have since died (the survivor intestate), leaving part of the estate unadministered, the Court will make a grant of administration (with the will annexed) of such unadministered estate to the residuary legatee or other person entitled thereto. (*See* Chapter 5.) It will, of course, be understood that all persons having a right prior to that of the applicant for the grant must be cleared off in the usual way.

The proposed Administrator may attend at the Registry and be sworn upon the original will or may be sworn upon the first grant or upon a sealed copy of the will. An office copy of the Act of the first grant must be lodged with the papers. The engrossment of the will should not contain the Act of the first grant.

The grant issues in respect of the *unadministered* assets, and these assets only must be brought into the Affidavit for Inland Revenue and the gross amount thereof given in the oath.

The papers required are the Oath, Inland Revenue Affidavit and Bond.

[*Form of oath to lead grant of administration (will)* de bonis
non *to residuary legatee.*]

In the High Court of Justice.

PROBATE, DIVORCE AND ADMIRALTY DIVISION.
(PROBATE.)

THE   REGISTRY.

IN the goods of   deceased.

I,   of   *widow*, make oath and say as
follows :—

1. That   of   (trade), deceased, died
on the   day of   18 , at
[having at the time of his death a fixed place of abode at   aforesaid,
within the district of the county of   ], and having made and duly
executed his last will and testament, and thereof appointed *his son*,   sole
executor.

2. That in month of   18 , the said   duly
proved the said will in this Division at the   Registry thereof,
and for some time intermeddled in the personal estate of the said testator and afterwards died, to wit, on the   day of   18 , intestate,
leaving part thereof unadministered.

3. That I believe the [paper] writing hereto annexed and marked by me to contain
the true [and original] last will and testament of the said testator; that I am the
relict of the said testator and the residuary legatee named in the said will; and
that I will well and faithfully administer the personal estate of the said testator
left unadministered as aforesaid, by paying his just debts and the legacies contained in
his said will, and distributing the residue of his estate according to law ; that I will
exhibit a true and perfect inventory of the said estate so left unadministered as
aforesaid, and render a just and true account thereof whenever required by law so to
do, and that the gross value of the whole of the personal estate of the said testator
left unadministered as aforesaid, is [*insert exact gross value of estate left unadministered*],
and no more, to the best of my knowledge, information and belief.

Sworn, &c.

[*Grant to representative of sole executor and sole residuary
legatee.*]

(USUAL HEADING.)

I,   of   , make oath and say as follows :—

1. That   of   , deceased, died on the
day of   18 , at   , having made and duly executed
his last will and testament, and thereof appointed his daughter
(spinster), sole executrix and sole residuary legatee.

2. That in the month of   18 , the said   duly
proved the said will in this Division at the   Registry thereof, and
for some time intermeddled in the personal estate of the said testator, and afterwards
died, to wit, on the   day of   18 , intestate, leaving part
thereof unadministered.

3. That I am the administrator of the personal estate of the said deceased, letters of administration of her personal estate having been granted to me by this Division at the   Registry thereof on the   day of 18   .

4. That I believe the [paper] writing hereto annexed and marked by me to contain the true last will and testament of the said testator; that I will well and faithfully administer, etc. [*and so on to end as in preceding form*].

[N.B.—The leading grant must be produced.]

[*Grant to residuary legatee on death of residuary legatee for life.*]

(USUAL HEADING.)

I,   of   , make oath and say as follows:—

1. That   of   deceased, died on the   day of   18   , having made and duly executed his last will and testament and thereof appointed his wife,   widow, sole executrix and residuary legatee for life.

2. That in the month of   18   , the said   duly proved the said will in this Division at the   Registry thereof, and for some time intermeddled in the personal estate of the said testator and afterwards died, to wit, on the   day of   18   , intestate, leaving part thereof unadministered.

3. That I am the lawful daughter of the said testator and one of the residuary legatees substituted in his said will.

4. That I believe the [paper] writing, &c. [*and so on as in preceding form.*]

[*Oath for legatee for life on renunciation of representative of residuary legatee.*]

(USUAL HEADING.)

I,   of   make oath and say as follows:—

1. That   of   deceased, died on the   day of   18   , at   , having made and duly executed his last will and testament, and did thereby appoint his brothers   and   executors, who duly proved the said will in this Division at the   Registry thereof, in the month of   18   .

2. That the said   and   for some time intermeddled in the personal estate of the said testator, and are both since dead, leaving part of the said estate unadministered.

3. That the said   survived his said co-executor and died on the   day of   18   , intestate.

4. That the said testator appointed   his sole residuary legatee, who survived the said testator and died on the   day of 18   , intestate.

5. That in the month of   18 , letters of administration of
the personal estate of the said   deceased, were granted by this Division
at the   Registry thereof, to   his lawful widow and relict,
who has duly renounced letters of administration (with the said will annexed) of the
personal estate of the said testator, left unadministered as aforesaid.

6. That I believe the [paper] writing hereto annexed and marked by me to contain
the true last will and testament of the said   deceased.

7. That I am the lawful niece and a legatee for life named in the said will; that I
will well and faithfully administer, etc., etc. [*as in preceding form*].

[N.B.—The grant to the renunciant must be produced.]

For Affidavit for Inland Revenue, *see* Chapter 3, and as to
duty-paid stamp on such Affidavit, *see* page 38.

Bond, *see* Chapter 7.

The seal fees payable, if no stamp duty has been paid, are
as follows:—

If the personal estate is under the value of—

	s.	d.
£100 ...	1	0
£200	3	0
£300	7	6
£450 ...	12	0
Above £450	12	6

ADMINISTRATIONS *DE BONIS NON.*

When a person to whom a grant of administration has
been made dies, leaving part of the estate unadministered,
the Court will make a grant of administration to any one
or more of the surviving next-of-kin, or, failing them, to
any one or more of other persons entitled in distribution.
All prior rights to that of the applicant for the grant
must be cleared off.

Grant will issue to the representative of a deceased next-of-
kin, or of a person entitled in distribution, if all the *living*
next-of-kin, or persons entitled, are dead or renounce.

The papers required are the Oath, Inland Revenue
Affidavit, Bond and office copy Act of first Grant.

H

[*Oath to lead grant of administration* de bonis non *to the son of intestate.*]

In the High Court of Justice.

PROBATE, DIVORCE AND ADMIRALTY DIVISION.
(PROBATE.)

THE   REGISTRY

     IN the goods of   deceased.

I,   of   (trade)
make oath and say:—

     1. That   of   (trade)
deceased, died on the   day of   18 , at   ,
intestate ; that in the month of   18 , letters of administration of the
personal estate of the said intestate were, by the authority of this Division at the
        Registry thereof granted to   *his lawful widow and relict*,
who for some time intermeddled in the said personal estate, and afterwards died, to
wit, on the   day of   , 18 , leaving part thereof
unadministered.

     2. That I am the natural and lawful son and one of the next-of-kin of the said
intestate ; that I will faithfully administer the personal estate of the said intestate left
unadministered as aforesaid, by paying his just debts and distributing the residue of
his said estate according to law ; that I will exhibit a true and perfect inventory of
the said estate, and render a just and true account thereof whenever required by law
so to do ; and that the gross value of the whole of the personal estate of the said
intestate left unadministered as aforesaid is (*insert exact gross value of unadministered
estate*) and no more, to the best of my knowledge, information and belief.

     Sworn, &c.,

[*Oath for grant to other next-of-kin.*]

(Usual Heading.)

I,   of   make oath and say:—

     1. That   of   deceased died on the
day of   18 , at   a widower and intestate ; that in the
month of   18 , letters of administration of the personal estate of the
said deceased, were by the authority of this Division at the   Registry
thereof granted to   his natural and lawful son and one of his next-of-
kin, who for some time intermeddled in the said personal estate and afterwards died, to
wit, on the   day of   18 , leaving part thereof unadministered.

     2. That I am the natural and lawful son and one other of the next-of-kin of the
said deceased ; that I will faithfully administer, etc. [*and so on to the end as in preceding
form.*]

[*Oath for grant to sister on death of mother who administered.*]

(USUAL HEADING.)

I,   of   make oath and say:—

1. That   of   deceased, died on the day of   18   , at   , a bachelor without a father and intestate ; that in the month of   18   , letters of administration of the personal estate of the said deceased were by the authority of this Division at the   Registry thereof, granted to   widow, his natural and lawful mother and only next-of-kin, who for some time intermeddled in the said personal estate and afterwards died, to wit, on the   day of   18   , leaving part thereof unadministered.

2. That I am the natural and lawful sister of the said deceased : that I will faithfully administer, etc. [*and so on to the end as in preceding form.*]

[*Oath for grant to person entitled in distribution on death of next-of-kin.*]

(USUAL HEADING.)

I,   of   , make oath and say:—

1. That   of   deceased, died on the   day of   18   , a bachelor without a parent and intestate ; that in the month of   18   , letters of administration of the personal estate of the said deceased were, by the authority of this Division at the   Registry thereof granted to *A. B.*, the natural and lawful brother and one of the next-of-kin of the said deceased, who for some time intermeddled in the said personal estate and afterwards died, to wit, on the   day of   18   , leaving part thereof unadministered.

2. That   the natural and lawful brother and the only other next-of-kin of the said deceased died in the lifetime of the said *A. B.*, deceased, to wit, on the   day of   18   [*or* survived the said *A. B.*, deceased, and is since dead without having taken upon himself letters of administration of the personal estate of the said deceased.]

3. That I am the lawful nephew and one of the persons entitled in distribution to the personal estate of the said deceased, being the natural and lawful son of the natural and lawful brother also of the said deceased who died in his lifetime, to wit, on the   day of   18   ; that I will faithfully administer, etc. [*and so on to the end as in preceding form.*]

For Inland Revenue Affidavit, *see* Chapter 3 ; as to duty paid stamp on affidavit, *see* page 38.

For Bond A. B., *see* Chapter 7.

The seal fee, where the effects are under £300, is the same as on the first grant, but where the effects amount to or exceed £300, the seal fee is 12s. 6d.

In other respects the fees and procedure are similar to the application for a grant of administration (will) *de bonis non*.

CHAPTER 14.

EXEMPLIFICATIONS, RENUNCIATIONS, NOTING DOMICILE, DUPLICATE GRANTS, RE-SEALING.

EXEMPLIFICATIONS of grant of probate (or letters of administration) for use in recovering property in the British Colonies or elsewhere out of the jurisdiction of the Court can be obtained on application for them. These exemplifications are written on parchment, and recite the grant, etc., with a copy of the will in the prescribed form, and issue under the seal of the Court. The fees are :—

Looking up original grant	..	..	£0	1	0
Duty on exemplification	..	..	3	0	0
Fee on exemplification	..	..	1	1	0
Engrossing ditto (1s. 6d. per folio).					

RENUNCIATION AFTER GRANT PASSED.

An executor to whom power has been reserved in a Grant of Probate to come in afterwards and prove may at any time renounce probate. The usual form of renunciation (*see* " Form of Renunciation," p. 137) with the addition of a clause reciting the grant to proving executor, is applicable for the purpose. The fees for recording it are 8s. 6d.

The grant must be produced, but the renunciation is not noted thereon. The fact of the filing is proved by obtaining an office copy of the renunciation, or of the Act of Probate.

NOTING DOMICILE WHEN GRANT PASSES.

When it becomes necessary to have the domicile of the deceased noted on a Grant of Probate or Administration, in order to deal with his personal property in Scotland, the ordinary form of oath to lead such grant should end thus :—

> "that   will exhibit a true and perfect inventory of all and singular the said estate and effects and render a just and true account thereof whenever required by law so to do; that the said deceased died domiciled in England and that the gross personal estate and effects of the said deceased in the United Kingdom is of the value of £
> and no more, to the best of my knowledge, information and belief."

The Inland Revenue affidavit should also show the particulars of the property in Scotland and in Ireland. When the grant passes, the Registrar will make a notation of domicile thereon, for which the additional fee of 5s. is charged.

NOTING DOMICILE *AFTER* THE GRANT HAS PASSED THE SEAL.

When, after a grant of probate or administration has passed the seal of the Court, it is found necessary that the domicile of the deceased should be noted on the grant in order to deal with the property in Scotland, the practitioner will furnish the Registrar with an affidavit *in duplicate* (*see* form p. 134), in order to lead the order for the notation to be made on the grant. The fees for the order are 7s.

The fee of 5s. is payable for making the notation, and 1s. for looking up the original grant.

DUPLICATE GRANTS.

A duplicate grant of probate or letters of administration with or without the will annexed may issue at any time after a grant has passed the seal of the Court.

The fees are somewhat similar to a double probate, and vary according to the length of the will.

No duplicate grants will issue to any applicant other than the acting executors, or one of them, or the administrators, or one of them (in case of a joint grant), or their solicitors furnished with a written authority under the hand of one of such executors or administrators, or their lawful attorney upon production of letter of attorney and filing a copy ; and if the application for a duplicate grant be not made within six months after the issue of the original grant, a written statement of the use to be made of the duplicate should be furnished by the applicant. The usual notation fee of 2s. 6d., and a further fee of 2s. 6d., for filing the written application or copy letter of attorney will be payable.

SCOTCH AND IRISH GRANTS.

In order to obtain the seal of the **English Court** to a Scotch or Irish grant the original grant must be produced and a copy filed. The copy to be filed may be on foolscap or brief sized paper.

The Scotch grant should show that there are English assets and should also state that the deceased died domiciled in Scotland.

In the case of an Irish grant a certificate from the Inland Revenue Officer in Ireland that duty has been paid on the English assets of the deceased must be produced and also, in cases of administration, a certificate from the Irish Court that sufficient security has been given.

If it is necessary to obtain the seal of the Irish Court to an English grant, the probate or letters of administration with a copy thereof and the necessary certificates and the fees may be deposited with the Registrar of the Principal or District Registry where the grant has been made, who will transmit the grant to Ireland for the purpose of re-sealing.

The fees payable are as follows :—

For affixing the seal to an Irish grant in order to its becoming in force for property in England :—

Effects in England:—	Probate.			Administration.		
	£	s.	d.	£	s.	d.
Under the value of £100	0	1	0	0	1	0
,, ,, ,, 200	0	3	0	0	4	6
,, ,, ,, 300	0	7	6	0	12	0
Above ,, ,, 300	0	12	6	0	12	6
For affixing the seal of the Court to an Irish grant taken under Section 16 of the Finance Act, 1894				0	2	6
For affixing the seal to an Irish grant taken under Section 33 of the Customs and Inland Revenue Act, 1881				0	15	0
For the Registrar's Fiat on an Irish grant ..				0	5	0
Filing stamp office certificate				0	2	6
Filing certificate as to bond				0	2	6
For affixing the seal of the Court to any confirmation of an executor issued by authority of a Commissary Court in Scotland				1	1	0
Collating confirmation or grant—						
If 10 folios of 90 words each, or under ..				0	2	6
Above 10 folios, per folio				0	0	3
Filing copy confirmation or grant				0	2	6
Search (per year)				0	0	6
Receipt for papers				0	1	0

In order to obtain the seal of the Irish Court to a grant issued by the English Court a certificate as to the payment of stamp duty and in case of administration a certificate of sufficient security must be obtained.

The former is issued by the Legacy Duty Office and the latter by the Probate Court.

If the deceased was trustee only of property in Ireland the following affidavit must be made :—

In the High Court of Justice.

PROBATE, DIVORCE AND ADMIRALTY DIVISION.
(PROBATE.)
THE   REGISTRY.

IN the goods of   deceased.

I,   of   , make oath and say as follows :—

1. That   of   deceased, died on the   day of   18 , at   , and probate of his will was granted to me this deponent the executor named in the said will on the   day of   18   , by this Division at the   Registry thereof.

2. That the said deceased was at the date of his death the sole surviving executor of the will of   of   deceased, who died on the   day of   18   , and whose will was proved at   on the   day of   18 .

3. That at the date of the death of the deceased there were standing in his name as such surviving executor of the will of the said deceased the following securities, namely :—

[*Give particulars and value at date of death.*]

4. That the said deceased was a trustee only of such securities and had not any beneficial interest therein nor had he any beneficial interest in any real or personal estate in Ireland.

5. That the said probate of the will of the said   deceased, is about to be resealed in the Probate and Matrimonial Division of the High Court of Justice in Ireland in respect of the said trust estate, and for this purpose it is desired to obtain from the Controller of Legacy and Succession Duties a certificate that Probate [or Estate] Duty is not payable in respect of such trust estate.

Sworn, etc.

If through inadvertence the fact that the estate included Irish assets is not stated in the affidavit for Inland Revenue, the Controller of Legacy Duty will not issue the stamp duty certificate until such mistake has been rectified by filing a statement in the form subjoined.

The statement may be signed by one of two or more executors or administrators.

In the High Court of Justice.

PROBATE, DIVORCE AND ADMIRALTY DIVISION.
(PROBATE).

THE   REGISTRY.

IN the goods of   deceased.

I,   of   , do hereby certify as follows :—

1. The said   of   deceased, died on the   day of   18   , at

2. That on the   day of   18   , probate of his will [or administration of his personal estate] was granted by this Division at the   Registry thereof, to me, the sole executor named in the said will [or the lawful widow and relict of the said deceased, *or as the case may be.*]

3. That in the affidavit filed on taking the said grant and dated the   day of   18   , I stated that the personal estate of the said deceased was of the gross value of £   , and that the whole of such personal estate was situate in England.

4. That the statement in such affidavit as to the situation of the said personal estate was through an oversight made in error and that as a matter of fact part of such personal estate, namely,   of the value of £   was situate in Ireland.

5. That I desire to have the true facts as to the situation of the said personal estate noted on the said Affidavit for Inland Revenue in order that I may obtain a certificate as to the payment of Estate [or Probate] Duty on the personal estate situate in Ireland.

(Signature.)

RE-SEALING OF COLONIAL PROBATES.

The Colonial Probates Act, 1892 (55 Vict. cap. 6) provides that where a Court of Probate in a British possession, to which the Act has been applied by an Order in Council, has granted (whether before or after the passing of the Act) probate or letters of administration in respect of the estate of a deceased person, such grant may, on being produced to a Court of Probate in the United Kingdom, be sealed with the seal of that Court, and thereupon shall have the same force and effect in the United Kingdom as if granted by that Court. The Act applies to any probate or letters of administration granted by a British Court in a foreign country.

The grant is not to be re-sealed until the Probate Duty (or Estate Duty, or other duty payable on the value of the estate and effects in the United Kingdom for which probate of administration is granted) has been paid; and, in the case of letters of administration, until security has been given sufficient in amount to cover the property in the United Kingdom to which the grant relates. The Court may also require evidence as to the domicile of the deceased. For the purposes of the Act a duplicate of any grant sealed with the seal of the Court granting same, or a copy thereof certified as correct by or under the authority of the Court granting the same, shall have the same effect as the original. By a Registrar's order exemplifications and copies which do not give a copy of the Act of Probate or Administration cannot be re-sealed.

Special or limited or temporary grants are not to be sealed except upon an order of one of the Registrars.

The practice on re-sealing is as follows :—

The application must be made in the Principal Registry by the executor or administrator, or by the attorney (lawfully authorized for that purpose) of such executor or administrator.

The power of attorney will be in the form given on page 136.

A notice of such application in the prescribed form must be inserted once in the *Times* newspaper, unless otherwise directed by the Registrars. The notice need not previously be submitted to the Registrars.

A copy of the grant to be re-sealed must be filed in the Registry ; such copy may be on foolscap or brief sized paper, and must include copies of all testamentary papers admitted to probate.

The oath of the executor, administrator or attorney must be in the prescribed form, *see* page 108.

In the case of application to re-seal letters of administration the applicant must give bond to cover the personal estate of the deceased within the jurisdiction of the Court of Probate. The form of bond is subjoined, and with regard to the sureties and penalty the practice given on page 63 is to be observed.

In every case and especially when the domicile of the deceased, as sworn to in the affidavit, differs from that suggested by the description in the grant, the Registrars may require further evidence as to domicile. If it should appear that the deceased was not at the time of death domiciled within the jurisdiction of the Court from which the grant issues the seal of the English Court is not to be affixed unless the grant is such as would have been made by the High Court of Justice in England.

When the application is made after the lapse of three years from the death of the deceased, a certificate of reason of delay must be filed (form on page 132).

The affidavit for Inland Revenue, if deceased died on or before 1st August, 1894, will be form "A"; if deceased died after that date will be form "A-1," *see* Chapter 3.

The places to which the Act has been extended by Order in Council are as follows:—

Cape of Good Hope	Western Australia
New South Wales	Ontario (Province)
Victoria	British Guiana
New Zealand	South Australia
Gibraltar	Straits Settlements
British Honduras	Tasmania
Hong Kong	Gold Coast Colony
Manitoba	Nova Scotia

British Columbia	Jamaica
Barbadoes	Lagos
Bahamas	Fiji
Trinidad and Tobago	Natal
Leeward Islands	North-West Territories
	(Canada).

The fees payable are as follows :—

	s.	d.
Receipt	1	0
Registering and Collating—3d. per folio of 90 words (minimum fee 2s. 6d.)		
Court Fee—as per scale on page		
Search—6d. per year from date of death.		
Certificate of Registrar	2	6
Registrar's Fiat	5	0
Filing Copy Grant	2	6
Filing Power of Attorney (if any)	2	6

The forms to be used are as follows :—

[*Oath.*]

In the High Court of Justice.

PROBATE, DIVORCE AND ADMIRALTY DIVISION.
(PROBATE.)

IN the goods of *A.B.*, deceased.

I, *C.D.* (or *E.F.*), of   make oath and say :—

1. That a grant of probate of the will (or letters of administration of the personal estate) of *A.B.*, late of   deceased, was granted to me (or *C.D.*) by the   Court at   on the   day of   18 .

2. That the said deceased was at the time of his death domiciled at   , [*the following words to be struck out if inapplicable*] within the jurisdiction of the said Court.

3. That the notice hereunder annexed was inserted in the *Times* newspaper on the   day of   18 .

4. That I am the attorney lawfully appointed of *C.D.*, under his hand and seal, and am duly authorised to apply to this Court for the sealing of the said grant. [*This paragraph to be struck out if inapplicable.*]

5. That the value of the personal estate in England amounts in value to the sum of   and no more, to the best of my knowledge, information, and belief.

Sworn, etc.

[*Advertisement.*]

A.B., deceased.

Notice is hereby given that after the expiration of eight days application will be made in the Principal Probate Registry of the High Court of Justice for the sealing of the probate of the will (or letters of administration of the personal estate) of A.B., late of   , deceased, granted by the   Court at on the   day of   18 .

Solicitors for

[*Administration bond (with or without will).*]

KNOW all men by these presents, that we, *A.B.*, of   , *C.D.*, of   , and *E.F.*, of   , are jointly and severally bound unto *G.H.*, the President of the Probate, Divorce, and Admiralty Division of Her Majesty's High Court of Justice, in the sum of   pounds, of good and lawful money of *Great Britain*, to be paid to the said *G.H.*, or to the President of the said Division for the time being, for which payment well and truly to be made we bind ourselves and each of us, for the whole, our heirs, executors, and administrators, firmly by these presents.

Sealed with our seals.

Dated the   day of   in the year of our Lord One Thousand Eight Hundred and Ninety   .

The condition of this obligation is such, that if the above-named *A.B.*, the administrator (with the will dated the   day of   , annexed) by authority of the   Court at   , acting under letters of administration granted to   on the   day of   , and now about to be sealed in England under the Colonial Probates Act, 1892, of the personal estate of *K.L.*, late of   deceased, who died on the   day of   18 , do, when lawfully called on in that behalf, make, or cause to be made, a true and perfect inventory of the personal estate of the said deceased in England which has or shall come to   hands, possession, or knowledge, or into the hands and possession of any other person for   , and the same so made do exhibit, or cause to be exhibited, into the Principal Probate Registry of Her Majesty's High Court of Justice, whenever required by law so to do, and the same personal estate do well and truly administer according to law; and further do make, or cause to be made, a true and just account of said administration, whenever required by law so to do, then this obligation to be void and of none effect, or else to remain in full force and virtue.

Signed, sealed, and delivered }
     by the within-named   }
                              }
in the presence of   }

A Commissioner for Oaths.

[Administration bond (with or without will) on application by attorney.]

KNOW all men by these presents, that we, *A.B.*, of   , *C.D.*, of   , and *E.F.*, of   , are jointly and severally bound unto *G.H.*, the President of the Probate, Divorce, and Admiralty Division of Her Majesty's High Court of Justice, in the sum of   pounds, of good and lawful money of *Great Britain*, to be paid to the said *G.H.*, or to the President of the said Division for the time being, for which payment well and truly to be made we bind ourselves and each of us, for the whole, our heirs, executors, and administrators, firmly by these presents. Sealed with our seals.

Dated the   day of   in the Year of our Lord One Thousand Eight Hundred and Ninety   .

The condition of this obligation is such, that if *K.L.*, of   , the administrator (with the will dated the   day of   , annexed), by authority of the   Court at   , acting under letters of administration granted to   on the   day of   , and now about to be sealed in England under the Colonial Probate Act, 1892, of the personal estate of *M.N.*, late of   deceased, who died on the   day of   18   , do, when lawfully called on in that behalf, make, or cause to be made, a true and perfect inventory of the personal estate of the said deceased in England which has or shall come to   hands, possession, or knowledge, or into the hands and possession of any other person for   , and the same so made do exhibit, or cause to be exhibited, into the Principal Probate Registry of Her Majesty's High Court of Justice, whenever required by law so to do, and the same personal estate do well and truly administer according to law ; and further do make, or cause to be made, a true and just account of   said administration, whenever required by law so to do, then this obligation to be void and of none effect, or else to remain in full force and virtue.

Signed, sealed, and delivered by the within-named ⎫
                                                  ⎬
in the presence of   ⎭

A Commissioner for Oaths.

CHAPTER 15.

ADDITIONAL SECURITY — ALTERATION IN GRANTS—VOLUNTARY REVOCATION OF GRANT—REGISTRAR'S FIAT —PROBATE REFUSED—CAVEATS.

ADDITIONAL SECURITY ON INCREASING THE AMOUNT OF AN ESTATE.

If it is discovered, after a grant of administration (with or without will annexed) has been made, that the amount given as the value of the estate was less than the true value thereof, by reason that some part of such estate was undervalued or by reason that additional assets have been ascertained, it will be necessary to pay additional Probate or Estate Duty by means of a corrective affidavit. The form " D " is to be used if the deceased died on or before the 1st August, 1894 ; if the deceased died after that date, form " D-1 " should be used. Before the Inland Revenue authorities will endorse on the Grant a certificate as to the payment of the additional duty, a certificate of additional security must be given, and a notation made on the Grant by the Registrar that full security has been given for the increased value of the estate. In order to obtain this certificate, an affidavit should be made by the administrator in the prescribed form (*see* page 124). A further certificate of delay is required in cases where a certificate was filed with the first grant. A new bond must also be given in double the amount of the additional assets. The interest of the administrator in the estate should be inserted in the bond which should be prepared as if for an original grant except that the word "intended" should be omitted.

The Rules applying to bonds for grant apply also to these cases. (*See* Chapters 7 and 9.)

The bond and affidavit will be filed with the original papers.

The fees are 12s. 6d. Should, however, the grant have been originally taken out under the 33rd Section of the Customs and Inland Revenue Act, 1881, or under the Finance Act, 1894, Section 16, and the value of the estate is afterwards sworn to exceed the sum of £300, or £500, as the case may be, payment is demanded of the full fees which would have been payable if the full gross value of the personal estate had been set forth when the grant issued. The same payment is demanded where the personal estate has originally been sworn to amount to a sum under or not exceeding £100. No credit can be taken in the former case for the fee of 15s. paid when the grant issued, as this is held to be forfeited.

If the parties object to the foregoing demand they will be called upon to furnish a statement in writing setting forth the nature and particulars of the additional property and the reason why it was not included in the original estimate of value brought in when the grant passed. The certificate will be withheld until the Registrars have considered such statement.

ALTERATIONS IN GRANT.

Any alteration that may be required to be made in a grant which has passed from any Registry can only be made therein by an order from one of the Principal Registrars. The order is founded upon an affidavit setting out the facts. If the application is made in the District Registry the alteration is made by the District Registrar on receipt of the order.

VOLUNTARY REVOCATION OF GRANT.

When by reason of errors in a grant or otherwise, it becomes necessary that the grant should be revoked, the practitioner will prepare an affidavit of the circumstances for the consideration of the Registrar of the Principal Registry, who will prepare and make the order, or require such further evidence as may be thought necessary. If the grant was taken in the District Registry the application to revoke must be made there, but the affidavit is to be headed " Principal Registry."

If the grant is to be revoked by reason of the discovery for the first time of a will ; or of a will of a later date than that proved, such will must be produced on filing the affidavit. The grant will be cancelled in the Principal Registry.

The special form of oath to lead the substituted grant cannot be sworn until the old grant has been cancelled. With the papers for the new grant must be filed a copy of the Act of the old grant having the order of revocation noted thereon. The affidavit for Inland Revenue will contain the assets as the same may be found with the value of same as at the date of the affidavit (Act of 1881), or their value at the death (Act of 1894), *see* Chapter 3. If the person applying for the second grant is the person who took the first grant the Inland Revenue authorities will grant a free mark, *see* page 38. If this is not the case duty must be paid by the applicant for the substituted grant, and the person to whom the grant was given in the first instance must make application to the Commissioners for return of the duty by means of a Corrective Affidavit.

The fees payable are the same as on an application for an original grant, but the search is made from the date of revocation.

I

The forms to be used are as follows :—

[Affidavit to lead Revocation of Probate, a later Will having been found.]

In the High Court of Justice.

PROBATE, DIVORCE AND ADMIRALTY DIVISION.
(PROBATE.)

THE PRINCIPAL REGISTRY.

IN the goods of   deceased.

I   of   make oath and say as follows :—

1. The said   of   deceased, died on the   day of
18   at   having duly made and executed a will bearing date
the   day of   18   whereof I the said   was appointed
the sole executor.

2. I verily believed (until I had as hereinafter deposed ascertained to the contrary)
that the said will was the last will and testament of   the said deceased,
and I applied to this Division at the   Registry, thereof, for and obtained
on the   day of   18   a grant of probate of the said will on the suggestion
that such will was the last will and testament of the said deceased.

3. That since the date last mentioned I have discovered [*state how*] a will duly
made and executed by the said deceased, of a later date than the date of the above-
mentioned will, to wit, a will bearing date the   day of   18   whereof
the said deceased appointed   sole executor, and whereby the said
deceased revoked all wills previously made by him.

4. I am therefore desirous that the probate, heretofore granted to me, shall be
revoked and declared null and void by this Division, and I have instructed
my solicitors, to pray and procure the said probate to be revoked, declared
null and void and cancelled accordingly.

Sworn, etc.

———————

[Affidavit to lead Revocation of Administration, a Will having been found.]

(USUAL HEADING.)

I   of   make oath and say as follows :—

1. The said   of   died on the   day of
18   at

2. I verily believed (until I had as hereinafter deposed ascertained to the contrary)
that the said deceased died intestate, and being the natural and lawful child and one
of the next-of-kin of the said deceased I applied to this Division at the
Registry thereof for and on the   day of   18   obtained therefrom
letters of administration of all and singular the personal estate and effects of the said
deceased, on the suggestion that he died intestate, a widower.

3. Since the date last mentioned [on looking through the papers and deeds of the
said deceased, *or as the case may be*] I found the original last will and testament of the
said deceased, which said will is duly made and executed by the said deceased and
bears date the   day of   18

4. [*State why search was not made earlier or other reasons why the will was not
discovered.*]

5. I am therefore desirous that the letters of administration granted to me, as
before stated, shall be revoked and declared null and void by this Division, and I have
instructed   , my solicitor, to pray and procure the said letters of
administration to be revoked, declared null and void and cancelled accordingly.

Sworn, etc.

[*Oath to lead Substituted Grant.*]

In the High Court of Justice.

PROBATE, DIVORCE AND ADMIRALTY DIVISION.
(PROBATE).

THE PRINCIPAL REGISTRY

IN the goods of   deceased.

I   of   make oath and say as follows :—

1. The said   of   deceased, died on the day of   18   , at   having made and duly executed his last will and testament, bearing date the   day of   18   , and thereof appointed me, *his brother*, this deponent, sole executor.

2. Notwithstanding the premises probate of an earlier will of the said testator, to wit, dated the   day of   18   , was on or about the   day of   18   , granted by this Division at the   Registry, thereof, to   the sole executor therein named.

[OR]

[2. Notwithstanding the premises letters of administration of the personal estate and effects of the said deceased, were on the   day of   18   , granted by this Division, at the   Registry thereof, to   the natural and lawful son and one of the next of-kin of the said deceased, on the suggestion that the said deceased died intestate, a widower]

3. The said grant of probate [*or* administration] has been since voluntarily brought in by or on the part and behalf of the said   and has been duly revoked and declared null and void to all intents and purposes in the law.

4. I believe the paper writing hereunto annexed and marked by me to contain the true and original last will and testament of the said deceased ; that I am the *brother* of the said deceased, and that I am the sole executor named in the said will ; that I will well and faithfully administer the personal estate of the said testator, by paying his just debts and the legacies contained in his will so far as the same shall thereto extend and the law bind me ; that I will exhibit a true and perfect inventory of all and singular the said estate and effects and render a just and true account thereof whenever required by law so to do ; and that the gross personal estate of the said testator is of the value of £   and no more to the best of my knowledge, information and belief.

     Sworn, etc.

REGISTRAR'S FIAT.

If there are alterations in a will which, by reason of their having been made, or, in the absence of evidence to the contrary, are presumed to have been made after execution, the will must be registered as it stood without such alterations, and the Registrar will require a copy of the will to be made in that state and filed with the papers, and will write upon such copy his fiat that the will is to be registered in accordance with such copy.

The fee of 5s. is charged for fiat, and 2s. 6d. for filing the copy. The fee for making the copy is 2s. 6d. for the first five folios, and 6d. for every additional folio.

PROBATE REFUSED.

When, by affidavit of the attesting witnesses, it is shown that a will was not executed in accordance with the requirements of the Wills Act, the Registrar will refuse probate thereof and mark the will accordingly. The fees are :—

Filing each affidavit	2s.
Registrar's fiat	5s.

Application can thereupon be made for a grant of letters of administration by the person entitled thereto.

CAVEATS.

If the practitioner is desirous of entering a caveat to prevent any grant issuing without notice to the caveator, he will attend at the Registry and fill up a form which is there provided for that purpose. The fee of 2s. 6d. is charged for entering the caveat.

Notice of such caveat having been entered will be transmitted from the District Registry to the Principal Registry, so that a record of the caveat remains in both registries. Should the deceased have residence in another district, notice is also sent to the Registry for such district, at the same time.

A caveat remains in force for six months only, but may be renewed from time to time.

Rule 62 provides that "no caveat shall affect any grant made on the day on which the caveat is entered, or on the day on which notice is received of a caveat having been entered in the Registry."

Such caveat may be withdrawn or subducted by the party who entered it, on payment of a fee of 2s. 6d., at any time before he is warned to enter an appearance to it, and notice of such withdrawal or subduction is sent to the Principal Registry, and also to the Registry of any other district in which the deceased may have had a fixed place of abode.

Should the party whose application is stopped by the caveat, be desirous that the caveat be cleared off, he will instruct his London agent accordingly, who will obtain from the Principal Registry a form of warning to be served upon the person who entered the caveat at the address therein given, and if no appearance be entered by or on behalf of the caveator after the service of the warning within the time therein limited, upon affidavits of the service of the warning and of search for and of no appearance thereto being entered in the books of the Principal Registry, a notice to that effect will be transmitted to the District Registrar, who will thereupon issue the grant to the party applying. A caveator may subduct his caveat within six days of the issuing of the warning.

A caveat cannot be warned from a District Registry.

CHAPTER 16.

FEES.

SEAL FEES.

		Probates.			Administrations.		
Net Estate sworn :—	£	£	s.	d.	£	s.	d.
Not to exceed -	100	0	1	0	0	1	0
Under - -	200	0	3	0	0	4	6
,,	300	0	7	6	0	12	0
,,	450	0	12	0	0	16	6
,,	600	0	16	6	1	2	6
,,	800	1	2	6	1	13	0
,,	1,000	1	13	0	2	5	0
,,	1,500	2	5	0	3	7	6
,,	2,000	3	0	0	4	10	0
,,	3,000	3	15	0	4	13	9
,,	4,000	4	10	0	4	17	6
,,	5,000	4	15	0	5	5	0
,,	6,000	5	0	0	5	12	6
,,	7,000	5	5	0	6	0	0
,,	8,000	5	10	0	6	7	6
,,	9,000	5	15	0	6	15	0
,,	10,000	6	0	0	7	2	6
,,	12,000	6	5	0	7	10	0
,,	14,000	6	10	0	7	17	6
,,	16,000	6	17	6	8	8	9
,,	18,000	7	5	0	9	0	0
,,	20,000	7	12	6	9	11	3
,,	25,000	8	2	6	10	6	3
,,	30,000	8	15	0	11	5	0
,,	35,000	9	7	6	12	3	9
,,	40,000	10	6	3	13	11	3
,,	45,000	11	5	0	15	0	0
,,	50,000	12	3	9	16	7	6
,,	60,000	13	2	6	17	16	3
,,	70,000	15	0	0	20	12	6
,,	80,000	16	17	6	23	8	9
,,	90,000.	18	15	0	26	5	0
,,	100,000	20	12	6	29	1	3
,,	120,000	21	11	3	30	9	6
,,	140,000	23	8	9	33	5	9
,,	160,000	25	6	3	36	2	0
,,	180,000	27	3	9	38	18	3
,,	200,000	29	1	3	41	14	6
,,	250,000	30	18	9	44	10	9
,,	300,000	35	12	6	46	17	6
,,	350,000	40	6	3	49	4	6
,,	400,000	41	17	6	51	11	3
,,	500,000	43	8	9	53	18	3
,,	600,000	46	11	3	58	11	9
,,	700,000	49	13	9	63	5	3
,,	800,000	52	16	3	67	18	9
,,	900,000	55	18	9	72	12	3
,,	1,000,000	59	1	3	77	5	9

MISCELLANEOUS FEES.

	£	s.	d.
Receipt for papers	0	1	0
Registering and collating wills and other documents—			
If 3 folios of 90 words each, or under	0	4	6
Above 3 folios, per folio	0	1	6
Search for former grants—			
For every full year or part of a year which has elapsed since the deceased's death	0	0	6
Certificate of Registrar..	0	2	6
Filing every affidavit, except the oath for executor or administrator and affidavit for Inland Revenue	0	2	0
Filing certificate of reason of delay	0	2	6
Filing power of attorney	0	2	6
Filing renunciation	0	2	6
Noting on grant that testator or intestate died domiciled in England	0	5	0
Registrar's order, noting on record that renunciation filed after grant issued	0	5	0

SEARCH AND INSPECTION OF WILLS.

	£	s.	d.
For every search for will or grant of letters of administration or any document filed in a Registry, including the looking up and inspecting an original will before the same is registered, or a registered copy of a will or an administration act	0	1	0
For every third will or administration act looked up in addition to the above	0	1	0

£ s. d.

For looking up and inspecting an original will after the same is registered in addition to the fee for the search 0 1 0

For looking up and producing any document filed in a Registry other than an original will or administration act 0 1 0

OFFICE COPIES AND EXTRACTS.

There are three descriptions of office copies to be obtained, namely :—

1. Plain office copy.
2. Certified copy.
3. Certified copy under seal.

The cost of a plain office copy is 1s. for search, and 2s. 6d. for the first five folios of the will, and 6d. for each additional folio.

The cost of a certified copy is the same, with the addition of 2s. 6d. for first ten folios (or less), and 3d. for every additional folio, for collating and certificate, and an impressed duty of 1s.

The cost of an office copy under seal is the same as a certified copy, with the addition of 5s. for the seal fee.

OFFICE COPIES AND EXTRACTS.

£ s. d.

For every office copy or extract of a will, or probate, or administration act, or of any document filed or deposited in a Registry, if five folios of ninety words or under ..   0 2 6

If exceeding five folios of ninety words, for every additional folio or part of a folio 0 0 6

	£	s.	d.

If the will or other document is 200 years old
and five folios of ninety words or under   ..   0   5   0

    If exceeding five folios of ninety words,
      for every additional folio or part of a folio   0   0   9

If the office copy of a will or any part of a will
or other document is required to be made
facsimile, and such will or part of a will or
other document is two folios of ninety words
in length or under, in addition to the fee for
the copy   0   1   0

    If exceeding two folios of ninety words,
      for every additional folio or part of a folio   0   0   6

For copies of wills and other documents in
foreign languages made by persons specially
employed for that purpose, the charges of the
persons so employed will be taken in addition
to any other fees which may be payable in
respect of such copies.

If a copy is required to be printed (in addition to a manuscript copy for the printer, at 6d.
per folio of ninety words and collating) :—

    If twenty folios of ninety words or under   0 10   0
    For every additional folio or part of a
    folio   0   1   0

For office copy of a will, minute, order, decree,
or any document under seal of the Court for
which no other fee is payable :—

    For the seal in addition to the fee for the
    copy and collating   0   5   0

For copies of plans, drawings and armorial
bearings, etc., such fee as shall be determined
by the Registrar in each particular case.

COLLATING DOCUMENTS.

£ s. d.

For collating copy of a probate and will, or copy of letters of administration with or without the will annexed, or any other instrument to be filed or deposited in the Registry, or for collating any copy or instrument with an original document already filed or deposited in the Registry, including the Registrar's certificate in verification thereof.

	£	s.	d.
If ten folios of ninety words each, or under	0	2	6
If above ten folios of ninety words each per folio	0	0	3

If there is any pencil writing copied, or the copy or any part thereof is *facsimile* in addition to the above fees :

	£	s.	d.
If such pencil writing or *facsimile* copy is two folios of ninety words in length or under	0	0	6
For every additional folio or part of a folio	0	0	3

ATTENDANCES.

If a practitioner desires the production of any original document filed in the Registry at any Assize or County Court, etc., he should give as much notice as possible to the Registrar (in no case less, *if possible*, than one day), in order that copies of such documents may be made and examined, according to the requirements of the Court, before such documents are taken out of the Registry.

	£	s.	d.
For any officer attending as a Witness, or to produce any records or documents to be given in evidence in any Court beyond three miles from the Registry, in addition to the reasonable expenses of the officer, for each day or part of a day he shall be necessarily absent from his office	1	1	0

Within three miles of the Registry :—	£	s.	d.
For the first day	1	1	0
For each subsequent day in the same sittings	0	10	6

TRANSMISSION OF ORIGINAL WILLS.

The President has recently directed that any original will, testamentary document, or script, whether before or after probate, and whether in an action or not and including wills brought in on subpœna, deposited for safe custody in the testator's lifetime, and lodged by the Lunacy Commissioners, may be sent in a registered cover by post to and from the Principal and District Registries.

An examined copy must take the place of the document sent.

FEES ON OATHS.

The fee of 1s. 6d. is charged for each oath made by any person duly entitled, and 1s. for marking each exhibit, whether on the same sheet of paper or not. No fee is charged for swearing the papers when application is made under the 33rd section, 44 Vic. c. 12, or 16th section of Finance Act, 1894.

REGISTRY FEES ON ATTESTING BONDS.

The fees for superintending and attesting the execution of a bond is 1s. 6d., and for each subsequent attestation 1s.

PRINTED CALENDARS.

Each Registry is supplied with printed calendars, containing particulars of all wills proved or letters of administration granted in England and Wales since the commencement of the Court of Probate Act, 1858. These calendars are intended for the use of the public on the usual search fee being paid.

CHAPTER 17.

FORMS.

[Affidavit for increasing the amount of an estate.]   Page 111.

In the High Court of Justice.

PROBATE, DIVORCE AND ADMIRALTY DIVISION.
(PROBATE.)

THE   REGISTRY.

IN the goods of   deceased.

I,   of   (trade), make oath and say that on
the   day of   18 , letters of administration of the personal
estate of the said   of   deceased were granted to me as (here insert
character in which deponent took the grant) of the said deceased, by the authority
of this Division at the   Registry thereof (as by the acts and records
thereof now remaining in the said District Registry will appear), and that
the said personal estate was then sworn to be of the gross value of £   s.   d.
and no more.

And I further make oath and say that it has since been discovered that the
said personal estate exceeds the said sum of £   s.   d.   ,being of
the gross value of £   s.   d.   and no more.

Sworn, etc.

[Affidavit for increasing the amount of an estate de bonis non.]*

(HEADING AS ABOVE.)

I,   of   make oath and say that on the   day of
18 , letters of administration [with the will annexed] of the personal estate of
the said   of   deceased, were granted to me, this deponent,
in this Division, at the   Registry thereof, I having previously made oath
that the whole of the personal estate of the said deceased left unadministered was
of the gross value of £

And I further make oath and say that it has since been discovered that the
personal estate of the said deceased left unadministered exceeds in value the sum
of £   and is of the gross value of £

Sworn, etc.

---

*[Affidavit for increasing the amount of an estate, before application
for grant* de bonis non.]*   Page 111.

(USUAL HEADING.)

IN the goods of *A.B.*, deceased.

I, *C.D.* of   (trade), make oath and say that in the month
of   18 , administration of the personal estate of the said *A.B.*,
of   (trade), deceased, was granted to   as (here
insert character in which the deceased administrator took the grant) of the said
deceased, by the authority of this Division, at the   Registry
thereof (as by the acts and records now remaining in the said
Registry will appear), and that the said personal estate was then sworn to be of
the value of £   s.   d.   , and no more.

And I further make oath and say, that the said   for some
time intermeddled in the said personal estate, but is since dead, to wit, on the
day of   18 , leaving part thereof un-
administered.

And I further make oath and say, that it has since been discovered that the
said personal estate exceeds the said sum of £   s.   d.   , being of the value
of £   s.   d.   , and no more.

And I lastly make oath and say, that I am (here insert character in which the
de bonis non grant will be taken) of the said *A.B.*, deceased, and am about to apply
for administration of the said personal estate left unadministered as aforesaid to
be granted to me.

Sworn, etc.

[Affidavit of attesting Witness verifying alterations in a will (or codicil).]

Page 4.

In the High Court of Justice

PROBATE, DIVORCE AND ADMIRALTY DIVISION.
(PROBATE.)

THE   REGISTRY.

(1) Insert name, residence and addition of the deponent.

IN the goods of   deceased.

(2) *Or* "do solemnly, sincerely, and truly affirm and declare."

I (¹)   make oath and say (²) that I am one of the

(3) "Codicil to the" *or* "to the first, second, third, etc., codicil to the" *as the case may be.*

subscribing witnesses to the (³)   last will and testa-

(4 & 5) Insert name, residence and addition of deceased.

ment of (⁴)   of (⁵)   deceased,

(6) "Will" *or* "codicil."

the said (⁶)   being now hereunto annexed, and bearing

(7) "Will" *or* "codicil."

date the   day of   One thousand

(8) "Signing h   name" *or* "making h   mark."

eight hundred and   : and that the said testat

(9) *or* "in the testimonium clause thereof," *or* "in the attestation clause thereto," *as the case may be, followed, in either of these cases, by these words, "meaning and intending such recited signature in final and due execution of his said Will."*

executed the said (⁷)   on the day of the date thereof

by (⁸)   at the foot or end thereof (⁹)

as the same now appears thereon, in the presence of me and of (¹⁰)

(10) Insert name or names of the other subscribing witness or witnesses.

the other subscribed witness (¹¹)

(11) *or* "witnesses"

thereto (¹²)   of us being present at the same time, and

(12) "both" *or* "all."

(13) "Will" *or* "codicil."

we thereupon attested and subscribed the said (¹³)   in

(14) "Will" *or* "codicil." *Specify* ALL *the interlineations, interpolations, obliterations, erasures and words written on erasures, and name the pages and the lines in (or between) which they occur,*

the presence of the said testat

And having particularly observed the following alteration

appearing in the said (¹⁴)   namely, the

(15) "Was" *or* "were all."

I further make oath and say that the said recited alteration (¹⁵)

(16) "Will" *or* "codicil."

made and written in the said (¹⁶)

(17) In case the alterations were made *after* execution, strike out from 15 and insert "were not made and written in the said will as the same now appear previously to the execution thereof, but at some period subsequent thereto."

as the same now appear previously to the execution thereof (¹⁷)

NOTE.—*If execution was by making a mark the last clause given in the form on page 127 must be added.*

Sworn by the said

at

on the   day of }

Before me

Or style of other person authorised to administer oaths under the Act.

A Commissioner for oaths.

N.B.—The following exhibit, to be signed by the Commissioner, to be put on the will (or codicil) referring to this affidavit :—" This is the testamentary paper writing, or will, referred to in the annexed affidavit of   sworn on the   day of   18

Before me

A.B.

A Commissioner, etc."

(*See* page 40.)

[Affidavit of attesting Witness in proof of the due execution of a will or codicil dated after 31st December, 1837.]   Page 2.

In the High Court of Justice.

PROBATE, DIVORCE AND ADMIRALTY DIVISION.
(PROBATE.)

THE   REGISTRY.

IN the goods of   deceased.

Insert the name, residence, title, profession, business, or addition of the deponent.

I   of

1. *Or* "do solemnly, sincerely, and truly affirm and declare" that, etc.

make oath (¹) that I am one of the subscribing witnesses to the (²)

last will and testament of

2. *Or* "to the codicil to the" *or* "the first, second, etc., codicil to the" last will, etc., as the case may be.

of (³)   deceased, the said (⁴)

3. Insert name, residence, title, profession, business, or addition of deceased.

Or "formerly of," etc., "but late of," etc.

being now hereunto annexed, bearing date the   day of

One thousand eight hundred and

4. "Will" *or* "codicil."

and that the said testat   executed the said (⁵)

5. "Will" *or* "codicil."

on the day of the date thereof, by signing his name at the foot or end

6. *Or* "in the testimonium clause thereof" *or* "in the attestation clause thereto," as the case may be, followed in either of these cases by these words, "meaning and intending such recited signature in final and due execution of his said will."

thereof (⁶)   as the same now appears thereon, in the

presence of me and of   the other subscribed

witness thereto, (⁷)   of us being present at the same time, and

7. "Both" *or* "all."
8. "Will" *or* "codicil."

we thereupon attested and subscribed the said (⁸)

in the presence of the said testat

NOTE.—*If execution of the will was by mark, form on page 127 must be used.*

Sworn at

on the   day of

18

Before me,

A Commissioner for oaths.

N.B.—The following exhibit clause, to be signed by the Commissioner, to be put on the will or codicil: "This is the testamentary paper writing, or will, referred to in the annexed affidavit of   sworn on the   day of   18   ."

Before me

A. B.,

A Commissioner, etc.

(*See* page 40.)

[*Affidavit of attesting Witness as to a testator's knowledge of the contents of his will (or codicil).*] Page 2.

In the High Court of Justice.

PROBATE, DIVORCE AND ADMIRALTY DIVISION.
(PROBATE.)

THE   REGISTRY.

IN the goods of   deceased.

(1) Insert name, residence and addition of deponent.

1 (¹)

(2) *Or* "do solemnly, sincerely, and truly affirm and declare."

make oath and say (²) that I am one of the subscribing witnesses to

(3) "Codicil to the " *or* "to the first, second, third, etc., codicil to the" *as the case may be.*

the (³)   last will and testament of (⁴)

of (⁵)   deceased, the said (⁶)

(4 & 5) Insert name, residence and addition of the deceased.

being now hereunto annexed, and bearing date the

(6) "Will" *or* "codicil."

day of   One thousand eight hundred and

(7) "Will" *or* "codicil."

and that the said testat   executed the said (⁷)

(8) "Signing h name," *or* "making h mark."

on the day of the date thereof by (⁸)   at the foot or

(9) *Or* "in the testimonium clause thereof," *or* "in the attestation clause thereto," *as the case may be,* followed in either of these cases by these words "meaning and intending such recited signature in final and due execution of his said will."

end thereof (⁹)   as the same now appears thereon, in

the presence of me and of (¹⁰)   the other subscribed

witness (¹¹)   thereto (¹²)   of us being present at

the same time, and we thereupon attested and subscribed the

said (¹³)   in the presence of the said testat

(10) Insert name or names of the other subscribing witness or witnesses.

(11) *Or* "witnesses."

(12) "Both" *or* "all."

(13) "Will" *or* "codicil."

And I further make oath and say, that previously to the execution

of the said (¹⁴)   by the said testat   the same was

(14) "Will" *or* "codicil."

read over to h   by (¹⁵)   and   he the said testat

(15) "Me" *or* "by A.B., in my presence."

at such time seemed thoroughly to understand and approve of the

(16) "Will" *or* "codicil."

contents of h   said (¹⁶)

Sworn by the said
at   on the
day of   , 18

Or style of other person authorised to administer oaths under the Act.

Before me,

A Commissioner for oaths.

N.B.—The following exhibit clause, to be signed by the Commissioner, to be put on the will (or codicil) referring to this affidavit : "This is the testamentary paper writing or will referred to in the annexed affidavit of   sworn on the   day of   , 18 ."
Before me,
A. B.,
A Commissioner, etc.

(*See* page 40.)

[*Affidavit to lead Registrar's Order assigning a guardian of an infant to take grant.*]   Page 71.

In the High Court of Justice.

PROBATE, DIVORCE AND ADMIRALTY DIVISION.
(PROBATE.)

THE PRINCIPAL REGISTRY.

IN the goods of   deceased.

I   of   make oath and say as follows : —

1. That the said   of   deceased, died at   on the day of   18   , intestate, a widower, leaving   spinster, his natural and lawful and only child, who is now an infant, to wit, of the age of four years and upwards, but under the age of seven years, and who, as I am advised, is therefore by law incapable of acting in her own name, and of electing a guardian to act on her part and behalf, and that there is no testamentary or other lawfully appointed guardian of the said infant.

2. I am the lawful grandfather and one of the next-of kin of the said infant, and I am ready and willing to undertake the guardianship of the said infant for the purpose of taking letters of administration of the personal estate of the said deceased, for the use and benefit of the said infant until she shall attain the age of twenty-one years.

Sworn at, etc.

[*Affidavit as to Identity of Executor.*]   Page 6.

In the High Court of Justice.

PROBATE, DIVORCE AND ADMIRALTY DIVISION.
(PROBATE.)

THE   REGISTRY.

IN the goods of   deceased.

I   of   make oath and say as follows :—

1. The said   of   deceased, died on the day of   18   , at   having made and duly executed his last will and testament hereunto annexed bearing date the   day of   18   , and thereof appointed me, this deponent, sole executor.

2. That the said testator described me in his said will as his nephew, but as a matter of fact I am not the nephew of the deceased, but am the lawful nephew of the lawful wife of the said deceased.

3. That the said deceased in his lifetime always spoke of and referred to me as his nephew and that he during his lifetime informed me of his intention to appoint me executor of his will.

4. That I am well acquainted with the family and relatives of the said deceased, and that to the best of my knowledge and belief the said deceased has not and never had a nephew of the name of

5. That I am the only person of the name of   residing at   as described in the said will.

Sworn, etc.

[Affidavit as to validity of Scotch Copy Will which has not been confirmed.] Page 8.

(USUAL HEADING).

I   of   , Writer to the Signet in Scotland, make oath and say as follows :—

1. That I have full knowledge of the laws and constitutions of the Kingdom of Scotland and have perused the copy of the will of   of
deceased, now hereunto annexed, which will is on record in the books of the   for the county of   .

2. That the said will is duly made in accordance with and conforms to and is valid by the said laws and constitutions of Scotland.

3. That the said official copy hereunto annexed is by the said laws and constitutions equivalent in all respects to the original, and that such copy would be received in all Courts in Scotland as making faith in judgment equally with the original, and that confirmation by the Commissary Court of Scotland is granted on production of such official copy.

Sworn, etc.

[Affidavit as to validity of will.] Page 9.

(USUAL HEADING.)

I   of   [*description*] make oath and say as follows :—

1. That I am [*state qualification such as "advocate"*] and have full knowledge of the laws and constitutions of the Empire [*or Republic or as the case may be*] of

2. That I have perused the last will and testament of the said
of   deceased, now hereunto annexed, bearing date the   day of 18   , and I make oath and say that the said will is duly made in accordance with and conforms to and is valid by the said laws and constitutions of the said Empire of

Sworn, etc.

[Affidavit as to Lunacy.] Page 74.

(USUAL HEADING.)

We   of   physician and   of asylum attendant, respectively make oath and say as follows :—

1. And first I the said   make oath and say that (who is, as I am informed and verily believe, the natural and lawful father and next-of-kin of the said   spinster, deceased) has been for the period of   years last past attended by me in my professional capacity, he being an inmate of the   Lunatic Asylum, where he now is under the care of my co-deponent the said   and that the said   has been for many years and now is a person of unsound mind and totally incapable of managing his affairs or of doing any act or thing whatever which requires the exercise of judgment or thought and that he is not likely soon to recover the use of his mental faculties.

2. And I the said   make oath and say that I am an attendant at the said lunatic asylum where the said   is now under restraint and confined, and that the said   has been for the period of   years confined in the said lunatic asylum and has there been under my care by reason of the fact that he is a person of unsound mind and that he now is a lunatic and totally incapable of managing himself or his affairs.

Sworn, etc.

K

[*Affidavit of handwriting.*]   Page 4.

In the High Court of Justice.

PROBATE, DIVORCE AND ADMIRALTY SESSION.
(PROBATE.)

THE   REGISTRY.

IN the goods of   deceased.

I, *C. D.*, of   in the county of   (trade), make oath that I knew and was well acquainted with *A. B.*, of in the county of   (trade), deceased, who died on the   day of   18   at [and had at the time of his death a fixed place of abode at within the district of the county of   ] for many years before and down to the time of his death, and that during such period I have frequently seen him write, and also subscribe his name to writings, whereby I have become well acquainted with his manner and character of handwriting and subscription, and having now with care and attention perused and inspected the paper writing hereunto annexed, purporting to be and contain the last will and testament of the said deceased, bearing date the   day of   18 beginning thus "   " ending thus "   " and being thus subscribed " *A. B.* " [*or as the case may be*], I further make oath, that I verily and in my conscience believe the whole body, series and contents of the said will, together with the names " *A. B.*" subscribed thereto as aforesaid [or, as the case may be], to be of the true and proper handwriting and subscription of the said deceased.

Sworn, etc.   _____

[*Affidavit of justification of sureties.*]   Pages 61, 74.

In the High Court of Justice.

PROBATE, DIVORCE AND ADMIRALTY DIVISION.
(PROBATE.)

THE   REGISTRY.

IN the goods of   , deceased.

We, *A. B.*, of   (trade), and *C. D.*, of   (trade), jointly and severally make oath that we are the proposed sureties on behalf of *E. F.*, the intended administrator of all and singular the personal estate of   , of   (trade), deceased, in the penal sum of (*here insert full amount of bond, with shillings and pence, if any*), for his faithful administration of the said personal estate of the said deceased; and I, the said *A. B.*, for myself further make oath, that I am, after payment of all my just debts, well and truly worth in real and personal estate the sum of £   s.   d.*   ; and I, the said *C. D.*, for myself further make oath that I am, after payment of all just debts, well and truly worth in real and personal estate the sum of £   s.   d.*

Sworn by both the above-named deponents at on the   day of   18 Before me,

A Commissioner for oaths.

* The gross amount of the personal estate of the deceased.

[*Affidavit of plight and condition of and finding of will.*]　Page 5.

In the High Court of Justice.

PROBATE, DIVORCE AND ADMIRALTY DIVISION.
(PROBATE.)

THE　　　　　　　　REGISTRY.

IN the goods of　　　　　　　　　　　　　　　deceased.

I, C. D., of　　　　　　　in the county of　　　　　　(trade), make oath that I am the sole executor named in the paper writing now hereunto annexed, purporting to be and contain the last will and testament of *A. B.*, of (trade), deceased, who died on the day of　　　　18　, at　　　　　, [and had at the time of his death a fixed place of abode at　　　　, within the district of the county of　　　　], the said will bearing date the　　　　　day of 18　, and having viewed and perused the said will and particularly observed [*here describe the plight and condition of the will or any other matters requiring to be accounted for, and set forth the finding of the will in its present state, and, if possible, trace the will from the possession of the deceased up to the time of making the affidavit*], I, the deponent, lastly make oath that the same is now in all respects in the same state, plight and condition as when found by me [*or as the case may be*] as aforesaid.

Sworn, etc.

[*Affidavit as to British Status.*]　Page 9.

In the High Court of Justice.

PROBATE, DIVORCE AND ADMIRALTY DIVISION.
(PROBATE.)

THE　　　　　　　REGISTRY.

IN the goods of　　　　　　　　　　　deceased.

I,　　　　of　　　　　make oath and say as follows : (1) I am the sole executor named in the last will and testament of the said of　　　　　now hereunto annexed bearing date the　　day of　　18　.

(2) That the said will was made at　　　　(3) That the said deceased was a British subject and born of English parents at and that h　　domicil of origin was English.

Sworn at, etc.

[*Affidavit of search.*]   Page 8.

In the High Court of Justice.

PROBATE, DIVORCE AND ADMIRALTY DIVISION
(PROBATE.)

THE   REGISTRY.

IN the goods of   deceased.

I, *C. D.*, of   , in the county of   , make oath that
I am the sole executor named in the paper writing hereunto annexed, purporting
to be and contain the last will and testament of *A. B.*, of
deceased, who died on the   day of   18 , at   ,
[and had at the time of his death a fixed place of abode at   within
the district of   ], the said will beginning thus "   ,"
ending thus "   " and being thus subscribed "   ." And
referring particularly to the fact that the blank spaces originally left in the said
will for the insertion of the day and month of the date thereof have never been
supplied (or as the case may be). I further make oath, that I have made inquiry of
E. F., the solicitor of the said deceased, and that I have also made diligent and
careful search in all places where he, the said deceased, usually kept his papers of
moment and concern, and in his depositories, in order to ascertain whether he had
or had not left any other will, but that I have been unable to discover any such
will. And I lastly make oath, that I verily believe the said deceased died without
having left any will, codicil, or testamentary paper whatever, other than the said
will by me hereinbefore deposed of.

Sworn, etc.

_____

[*Affidavit of reason of delay.*]   Page 7.

(HEADING AS ABOVE.)

IN the goods of   deceased.

I,
the Party applying for
of
of
deceased, who died on the   18
make oath and say as follows:—

That the only personal estate and effects which the said deceased died
possessed of consisted of*

That I am now applying for the said
for the purpose only of

Sworn at, etc.

_____

[*Certificate of reason of delay.*]   Page 7.

(HEADING AS ABOVE.)

I   of   the party applying for probate of the will
[*or* administration of the personal estate] of   of
deceased, do hereby certify that the reason why I have not sooner applied for the
said probate [*or* administration] is that the only personal estate of which the said
deceased died possessed consisted of*
and that the said grant is now required for the purpose of
and for no other purpose.

(Signed)

I believe the above to be true.

(Signed)   solicitor.

* Particulars and value of the personal estate should be set out and if the estate to be
administered consists of a share under a will or intestacy full information and
dates of death should be given.

[*Caveat.*] Page 116.

In the High Court of Justice.

(PROBATE DIVISION.)

THE   REGISTRY.

deceased.

Insert name, residence, and title, profession, business, or addition of deceased. Here insert all references at date of death.

Let nothing be done in the goods of

of

Insert names, residences, and titles, professions, business, or additionals of Caveators.

deceased, who died on the   day of eight hundred and   , at time of   death a fixed place of abode at aforesaid, within the District of unknown to

of

One thousand [and had at the

]

having interest.

Dated   day of   18

(Signed)

[*Declaration of personal estate.*] Pages 71, 74.

In the High Court of Justice.

PROBATE, DIVORCE AND ADMIRALTY DIVISION.

(PROBATE.)

THE   REGISTRY.

IN the goods of   deceased.

A true declaration of all and singular the personal estate of *A. B.* of   (trade), deceased, who died on the day of   18   , at [having at the time of h   death a fixed place of abode at aforesaid, within the district of the county of   ], which has at any time since h   death come into the hands, possession or knowledge of *C. D.*, the intended administrator [or the intended administrator (with the will annexed)] of the said estate, made and exhibited upon and by virtue of the corporal oath of the said *C. D.*, follows, to wit :

First, this declarant declares that the said deceased was at the time of h death possessed of or entitled to —

(Here copy details from schedule of Inland Revenue Affidavit).

£

Lastly, this declarant saith that no personal estate of or belonging to the said deceased has at any time since h   death come to the hands, possession or knowledge of this declarant, save as is hereinbefore set forth.

On the   day of   18   , the said *C. D.* was duly sworn to the truth of the above declaration. at   in the county of

Before me,

A Commissioner, etc.

[*Oath of executor (or administrator), where the domicile is to be noted when grant passes.*]   Page 18.

In the High Court of Justice.

PROBATE, DIVORCE AND ADMIRALTY DIVISION.
(PROBATE.)
THE   REGISTRY.
IN the goods of   deceased.

I (here take in oath for executor (Chap. 2), or administrator (Chap. 9), as the case may be, until arriving at the words "whenever required by law so to do," *then follows*, that the said deceased died domiciled in England, and that the gross personal estate of the said testator [*or intestate*] in the United Kingdom is of the value of £   s.   d.   , and no more, to the best of my knowledge, information and belief.

Sworn, etc.

[*Affidavit to lead Principal Registrar's Order for notation of domicile after probate has passed the seal.*]   Page 101.

In the High Court of Justice.

PROBATE, DIVORCE AND ADMIRALTY DIVISION.
(PROBATE.)
THE   REGISTRY.
IN the goods of *A. B.*, deceased.

I,   of
in the county of   , make oath that
                                of
in the county of   deceased, died on the
day of   at   aforesaid
and was at the time of h   death domiciled in that part of the United Kingdom called England, and that
granted to me by the High Court of Justice at the
Probate Registry thereof at   on the
day of   and that the personal
estate of the said deceased which h   any way died possessed of or entitled to
within the United Kingdom of Great Britain and Ireland, and for or in respect of
which the said   granted
exclusive of what the said deceased may have been possessed of or entitled to as a Trustee for any other person or persons and not beneficially, but including all such personal estate as the said deceased under any authority entitling h   to dispose of the same as h   might think fit, has disposed of by h   said will, and without deducting anything on account of the debts due and owing from the said deceased were altogether of the gross value of £   and no more to the best of my knowledge, information and belief.

And I further make oath that a part of the said personal estate of the said deceased, of the value of £   was in England, and a further part thereof, amounting in value to the sum of £
and more particularly mentioned and set forth in the schedule hereunto annexed was in Scotland, and that the said deceased was   at the time of h   death possessed of or entitled to   personal estate in Ireland
to the best of my knowledge, information and belief.

Sworn, etc.
THE SCHEDULE REFERRED TO.
(Here set out particulars of personal estate in Scotland.)
A. B.   *C. D.*
Executor.   Commissioner.

[Election of Guardians—Administration.] Page 70.

In the High Court of Justice.

PROBATE, DIVORCE AND ADMIRALTY DIVISION.
(PROBATE.)

THE   REGISTRY.

IN the goods of   deceased

WHEREAS *A. B.,* of   in the county of
(trade), deceased, died on the   day of   18   at
a widower and intestate, [having at the time of his death a fixed place of abode
at   aforesaid, within the district of the county of
      ], leaving *C. D.,* spinster, *E. F.* and *G. H.,* his natural and lawful children,
and only next-of-kin, who are now in their minority and infancy respectively, to wit,
the said *C. D.* being a minor of the age of   years only, the said *E. F.*
being a minor of the age of   years only, and the said *G. H.* being an
infant of the age of   years only.

NOW we, the said *C. D.* and *E. F.,* do hereby make choice of and elect *I. J.,*
of   (trade), our lawful grandfather and only next-of-kin, to be our
curator and guardian for the purpose of taking out letters of administration of the
personal estate of the said intestate to be granted to him for our use and benefit
and until one of us shall attain the age of 21 years.

Signed by the said *C. D.* and *E. F.,* on ⎫
the   day of   ⎬
18   , in the presence of   ⎭

(Name, residence, and occupation of a disinterested witness.)

[Election of Guardian—Administration—Will.] Page 58.

(HEADING AS ABOVE.)

WHEREAS   of   deceased, died on the   day of
18   , at   having duly made and executed his last will and testament
bearing date the   day of   18   , and thereof appointed
and   who have duly renounced probate and execution thereof.

AND WHEREAS the said testator by his said will appointed his daughter
     spinster, his sole residuary legatee.

AND WHEREAS the said   is now a minor of the age of
years and upwards but under the age of 21 years.

NOW I the said   do hereby make choice of and elect
of   my lawful uncle, and one of my next-of-kin, to be my curator and
guardian for the purpose of taking out letters of administration (with the said will
annexed) of the personal estate of the said deceased to be granted to him for my use
and benefit and until I shall attain the age of 21 years.

Signed, etc.

[Power of attorney to take administration with will.] Page 60.

WHEREAS HENRY JONES, of the city and county of Newcastle-upon-Tyne, grocer, deceased, died on the 12th day of August, 1882, at Newcastle-upon-Tyne aforesaid, having at the time of his death a fixed place of abode at the city and county of Newcastle-upon-Tyne aforesaid, within the district of the county of Northumberland, having made and duly executed his last will and testament, bearing date the 15th day of July, 1882, and thereof appointed his nephews, William Jones and Thomas Jones, executors.

NOW, we the said William Jones, hotel-keeper, and Thomas Jones, hotel-keeper, at present residing at   in the city of Paris, in the Republic of France, do hereby nominate, constitute and appoint William Smith, of the city and county of Newcastle-upon-Tyne aforesaid, printer, to be our lawful attorney for the purpose of obtaining administration (with the said will annexed) of the personal estate of the said testator, to be granted to him for our use and benefit, and until we shall duly apply for and obtain probate of the said will to be granted to us; and we hereby promise to ratify and confirm whatever our said attorney shall lawfully do or cause to be done in the premises.

In witness whereof we have hereunto set our hands and seals, this 8th day of November, in the year of our Lord, 1882.

Signed, sealed and delivered by⎫
the said William Jones and ⎬
Thomas Jones in the presence ⎭
of

(L.S.)

[To be witnessed by one disinterested person who should add his address and occupation.]

[Power of attorney of next-of-kin of an intestate.] Page 73.

WHEREAS, ANDREW BROWN, of John Street, in the city of Durham, brewer, deceased, died on the 25th day of January, 1882, at John Street aforesaid, a bachelor and intestate, having at the time of his death a fixed place of abode at John Street aforesaid, within the district of the county of Durham, and leaving John Brown, his natural and lawful father, and next-of-kin, him surviving.

NOW, I, the said John Brown, at present residing at Ross, in the Province of Westland, in the Colony of New Zealand, miner, the natural and lawful father, and next-of-kin of the said intestate, do hereby nominate, constitute and appoint Thomas Smith, of the said city of Durham, draper, to be my lawful attorney for the purpose of obtaining letters of administration of the personal estate of the said intestate, to be granted to him for my use and benefit, and until I shall duly apply for and obtain letters of administration of the personal estate of the said intestate to be granted to me. And I hereby promise to ratify and confirm whatever my said attorney shall lawfully do or cause to be done in the premises.

In witness whereof I have hereunto set my hand and seal, this 5th day of March, in the year of our Lord, 1882.

Signed, sealed and delivered by the⎫
said John Brown in the presence ⎬
of ⎭

(L.S.)

[*Renunciation of probate and administration with the will annexed.*]

Page 46.

𝕴𝖓 𝖙𝖍𝖊 𝕳𝖎𝖌𝖍 𝕮𝖔𝖚𝖗𝖙 𝖔𝖋 𝕵𝖚𝖘𝖙𝖎𝖈𝖊.

PROBATE, DIVORCE AND ADMIRALTY DIVISION.

(PROBATE.)

THE   REGISTRY.

(1) Insert name only of deceased.

IN the goods of (¹)   deceased.

(2) Insert name, residence, title, profession, business or addition of deceased.

WHEREAS (²)   of (³)

died on the   day of   18 , at

(3) Or "formerly of," etc., "but of late," etc.

[having at the time of (⁴) h death a fixed place of abode at

aforesaid, within the district of the county of   ], having

(4) " His " *or* " her."

made and duly executed (⁵)   last will and testament (⁶)

(5) " His " *or* " her."

bearing date the   day of   18

(6) " With one codicil " or with " codicils " thereto as the case may be.

(⁷)   and thereof appointed *his* (here insert

relationship, if any) (⁸)   executor

(7) If any codicils their dates should be also inserted.

(⁹)

(8) Or, " and of his said will or codicil appointed," as the case may be.

NOW,   the said   (¹⁰) do hereby declare

that   have not intermeddled in the personal estate and effects of

(9) " And universal (or residuary) legatee in trust," as the case may be.

the said deceased, and will not hereafter intermeddle therein with

intent to defraud creditors, and   do hereby expressly renounce all

right and title to the probate and execution of the said will

(10) If the renunciant is a " widow," " spinster," or "wife of——," she should here be so described.

(¹¹)   (or *the Letters of Administration with the said will*

annexed, of the personal estate and effects of the said deceased, as the case

(11) " And codicils," if any.

may be).

Signed by the said   this }
      day of   18   in the }
   presence of

(One disinterested witness sufficient, who should add his residence and addition to his signature).

[*Renunciation of administration.*]   Page 68.

In the High Court of Justice.

PROBATE, DIVORCE AND ADMIRALTY DIVISION.
(PROBATE.)

THE   REGISTRY.

IN the goods of   deceased.

Insert name only of deceased.	WHEREAS of in the
[Insert the name, residence and title, profession, business or addition of the deceased, at full length.]	county of deceased, died on the day of
	18 , at intestate, (¹)
(1) "A bachelor," "spinster," "widower," *or otherwise.* To be varied according to the fact.	[having at the time of h death a fixed place of abode at aforesaid, within the district of the county of]
(2) "His natural and lawful child (or children), or one, two, etc., of his natural and lawful children, or we are his [*insert relationship*] and one, two, etc., of his next-of-kin," or otherwise, and showing his, her or their degree as kindred to the deceased. *See* Chap. 8 & 9.	leaving (name of renunciant) (²)
(3) If renunciant is a "widow," "spinster," or "wife of ," it must be here shown.	NOW the said (³)
	do hereby expressly renounce all right and title to letters
(4) If consent also required, insert, "and do also hereby expressly consent that letters of administration be granted to my [*here insert relationship*]."	of administration of the personal estate and effects of the said deceased. (⁴)

Signed by the said

this   day of   18   ,

in the presence of

(One disinterested witness sufficient,
who should add his residence and addition
to his signature.)

[*Renunciation of guardianship.*] Page 57.

In the High Court of Justice.

PROBATE, DIVORCE AND ADMIRALTY DIVISION.

(PROBATE.)

THE   REGISTRY.

IN the goods of   deceased.

WHEREAS   of   in the county of
deceased, died on the   day of
18   , at   [having at the time of his death a fixed place of abode
at   aforesaid, within the district of the county of   ]
having made and duly executed his last will and testament, bearing date the
day of   18   , and thereof appointed
sole executor and universal legatee, who is now in his minority, to
wit, a minor, of the age of   years only.

AND WHEREAS I, the undersigned   am the natural and
lawful   and only (or "one of the") next-of-kin of the said minor.

NOW I, the said   do hereby expressly renounce all my right and title
in and to the curation or guardianship of the said minor.

Signed by the said
on the   day of   18
(Name, residence and occupation of a disinterested witness.)

CHAPTER 18.

RULES, ORDERS AND INSTRUCTIONS

FOR THE

PRINCIPAL AND DISTRICT REGISTRARS

OF

HER MAJESTY'S COURT OF PROBATE,

Made under the Provisions of the Statutes 20 & 21 Vic.
c. 77, *and* 21 & 22 Vic. c. 95,

IN RESPECT OF

NON-CONTENTIOUS BUSINESS.

The following Rules apply to the Principal and District
Registries. The Principal Registry Rules took effect
on 1st September, 1862, and the District Registry Rules
on the 2nd day of March, 1863. The words specially
applicable to District Registries are in brackets.

NON-CONTENTIOUS BUSINESS shall include all
common form business as defined by the Court of Probate
Act, 1857, and the warning of caveats.

1 P.R. and 1 D.R.—*Application for probate or
letters of administration* may be made at the Principal
Registry in all cases. [Application may also be made at a
District Registry in cases where the deceased, at the time
of his death, had a fixed place of abode within the District
in which the application is made, and not otherwise.]

2 P.R. and 2 D.R.—Such applications may be made through a proctor, solicitor, or attorney, or in person by executors and parties entitled to grants of administration.

[**3 D.R.**—The District Registrar, before he entertains any application for probate or letters of administration, must ascertain that the deceased had, at the time of his death, a fixed place of abode within his district.]

3 P.R. and 4 D.R.—The [District] Registrar is not to allow probate or letters of administration to issue until all the enquiries which he may see fit to institute have been answered to his satisfaction, [and this refers more particularly to applications made in person by executors and others.] The [District] Registrar is, notwithstanding, to afford as great facility for the obtaining grants of probate or administration as is consistent with a due regard to the prevention of error or fraud.

[**5 D.R.**—No District Registrar or clerk in the District Registry shall directly or indirectly transact business for himself, or as the proctor or solicitor of any other person in the District Registry to which he has been appointed.]

AS TO PROBATE OF WILLS AND CODICILS AND LETTERS OF ADMINISTRATION WITH THE WILL [OR WILL AND CODICILS] ANNEXED. WHERE THE WILLS AND CODICILS ARE DATED AFTER 31st DECEMBER, 1837.

Execution of a will.

[**6 D.R.**—Upon receiving an application for probate or letters of administration with the will annexed, the District Registrar must inspect the will and each codicil, and see whether by the terms of the attestation clause (if any) it

is shown that the same have been executed in accordance
with the provisions of statutes 1 Vic. c. 26, and 15 Vic.
c. 24.]

4 P.R. and 7 D.R.—If there be no attestation clause in a
will or codicil presented for probate, or if the attestation
clause thereto be insufficient, the [District] Registrar must
require an affidavit from at least one of the subscribing witnesses, if they or either of them be living, to prove that the
provisions of 1 Vic. c. 26, s. 9, and 15 Vic. c. 24, in reference
to the execution were in fact complied with.

[7*a*. The practice of registering affidavits shall be dis-
continued, and in lieu thereof a note, signed by the District
Registrar, shall be inserted on the engrossed copy, will,
or codicil annexed to the probate or letters of administration,
and registered, to the effect that affidavits of due execution,
of domicile, or as the case may be, have been filed.
Provided, that in cases presenting difficulty the affidavits
themselves may still be registered, with the consent of a
Registrar of the Principal Registry.]

5 P.R. and 8 D.R.—If on perusing the affidavits of both
the subscribing witnesses it appear that the requirements of
the statute were not complied with, the [District] Registrar
must refuse probate.

6 P.R. and 9 D.R.—If on perusing the affidavit or affidavits setting forth the facts of the case, it appear doubtful
whether the will or codicil has been duly executed, the [Dis-
trict] Registrar [must transmit a statement of the matter to
the Registrars of the Principal Registry, who] may require
the parties to bring the matter before the Judge on motion.

7 P.R. and 10 D.R.—If both the subscribing witnesses
are dead, or if from other circumstances no affidavit can be
obtained from either of them, resort must be had to other

persons (if any) who may have been present at the execution
of the will or codicil ; but if no affidavit of any such other
person can be obtained, evidence on affidavit must be pro-
cured of that fact and of the handwriting of the deceased
and the subscribing witnesses, and also of any circumstances which may raise a presumption in favour of the
due execution.

Interlineations and alterations.

8 P.R. and 11 D.R.—Interlineations and alterations are
invalid unless they exist in the will at the time of its execution, or, if made afterwards, unless they have been executed
and attested in the mode required by the statute, or unless
they have been rendered valid by the re-execution of the
will, or by the subsequent execution of a codicil thereto.

9 P.R. and 12 D.R.—When interlineations and alterations appear in the will (unless duly executed, or recited in or
otherwise identified by the attestation clause), an affidavit or
affidavits in proof of their having existed in the will before
its execution must be filed, except when the alterations
are merely verbal, or when they are of but small importance and are evidenced by the initials of the attesting
witnesses.

Erasures and obliterations.

10 P.R. and 13 D.R.—Erasures and obliterations are not
to prevail unless proved to have existed in the will at the time
of its execution, or unless the alterations thereby effected in
the will are duly executed and attested, or unless they have
been rendered valid by the re-execution of the will, or by
the subsequent execution of a codicil thereto.   If no
satisfactory evidence can be adduced as to the time when

such erasures and obliterations were made, and the words erased or obliterated be not entirely effaced, but can upon inspection of the paper be ascertained, they must form part of the probate.

11 P.R. and 14 D.R.—In every case of words having been erased or obliterated which might have been of importance, an affidavit must be required.

Deeds, etc., referred to in a will.

12 P.R. and 15 D.R.—If a will contain a reference to any deed, paper, memorandum, or other document, of such a nature as to raise a question whether it ought or ought not to form a constituent part of the will, the production of such deed, paper, memorandum, or other document must be required, with a view to ascertain whether it be entitled to probate; and, if not produced, its non-production must be accounted for.

13 P.R. and 16 D.R.—No deed, paper, memorandum, or other document can form part of a will unless it was in existence at the time when the will was executed.

Appearance of the paper.

14 P.R. and 17 D.R.—If there are any vestiges of sealing wax or wafers or other marks upon the testamentary papers, leading to the inference that a paper, memorandum, or other document has been annexed or attached to the same, they must be satisfactorily accounted for, or the production of such paper, memorandum, or other document must be required; and, if not produced, its non-production must be accounted for.

Married woman's will.[*]

15 P.R. and 18 D.R.—In granting probate of a married woman's will, made by virtue of a power or administration with such will annexed, the power under which the will purports to have been made must be specified in the grant.

Codicils.

16 P.R. and 19 D.R.—The above rules and orders respecting wills apply equally to codicils.

Doubtful cases.

[**20 D.R.**—If it be doubtful whether any will or codicil be entitled to probate, or whether any interlineation, alteration, erasure, or obliteration ought to prevail, or whether any deed, paper, memorandum, or other document ought to form part of a will or codicil, or if any doubt arise in consequence of the appearance of the paper, or on any other point, the District Registrar must communicate with the Registrars of the Principal Registry.]

Letters of administration with will annexed.

[**21 D.R.**—The right of parties to letters of administration with the will annexed, and letters of administration with the will annexed *de bonis non*, depends so entirely upon the circumstances of each particular case, taken in connection with the wording of the will, that no general rules, other than those which have obtained a judicial sanction, can be laid down for the guidance of the District Registrars. Whenever the right of the party applying is at all questionable, a statement of the case, accompanied by a copy of the will, must be transmitted to the Registrars of the Principal Registry, who will advise thereon.]

[*] This rule is repealed by an Order dated the 29th day of March, 1887. (*See* Page 86.)

L

AS TO PROBATE OF WILLS, CODICILS AND TESTAMENTARY PAPERS RELATING TO PERSONALTY, AND DATED BEFORE THE 1st JANUARY, 1838.

Execution of a will.

17 P.R. and 22 D.R.—It is not necessary that a will, codicil, or testamentary paper dated before 1st January, 1838, should be signed by the testator or attested by witnesses to constitute it a valid disposition of a testator's personal property. Although neither signed by the testator nor attested by witnesses, it may nevertheless be valid; but in such cases the testator's intention that it should operate as his will, codicil, or testamentary disposition must be clearly proved by circumstances.

18 P.R. and 23 D.R.—A will, codicil, or testamentary paper, signed at the end of it by the testator, and attested by two disinterested witnesses (although there be no clause of attestation), is *primâ facie* entitled to probate.

19 P.R. and 24 D.R.—In cases where a will, codicil, or testamentary paper is attested by two witnesses, such witnesses are not required to have been present with the testator at the same time. It is sufficient if the testator subscribed his name or made his mark to it in the presence of one attesting witness, or produced it with his name already written or his mark already made, to one attesting witness, and afterwards produced it to the other attesting witness, provided that on each occasion he declared it to be his will, codicil, or testamentary disposition, or otherwise notified his intention that it should operate as such.

20 P.R. and 25 D.R.—If the will, codicil, or testamentary paper is signed at the end of it by the testator, but is unattested, and there is nothing to show an intention that it should be attested by witnesses, the affidavit of two disinterested persons, to prove the signature to be of the handwriting of the testator, will be sufficient to entitle the paper to probate.

21 P.R. and 26 D.R.—If the will, codicil, or testamentary paper is signed at the end of it by the testator, and attested by one witness only, and there is nothing to show the testator's intention that it should be attested by a second witness, the affidavit of one disinterested person, to prove the signature to be of the handwriting of the testator, will be sufficient to entitle the paper to probate.

22 P.R. and 27 D.R.—The circumstance of a person being named as an executor in the will, codicil, or testamentary paper, or being interested as a legatee, or as the husband or wife of a legatee under such will, codicil, or testamentary paper, rendered him or her incompetent to become an attesting witness to it, so that if the name of a person so interested appears as that of a subscribing witness to the will, codicil, or testamentary paper, the same, so far as regards his or her attestation, must be considered as unattested, and his or her evidence in support thereof will be inadmissible unless he or she shall first release his or her interest thereunder.

23 P.R. and 28 D.R.—[The will, codicil, or testamentary paper should appear on the face of it to be a complete document;] if an attestation clause or the word "witnesses" appear written at the foot of the paper, the same being unattested, or if the paper purport on the face of it to be a draft of a will, the copy of a will, or instructions for a will, it must *primâ facie* be considered as an incomplete paper, and not, save under special circumstances, entitled to probate.

L 2

Appearance of paper.

24 P.R. and 29 D.R.—Any appearance of an attempted cancellation of a testamentary paper by burning, tearing, obliteration or otherwise, and every circumstance leading to a presumption of abandonment or revocation of such a paper on the part of the testator must be accounted for [or explained by affidavits. In such cases the testamentary paper and the evidence taken in support of it should be transmitted to the Registrars of the Principal Registry.]

Alterations and interlineations.

25 P.R. and 30 D.R.—Alterations and interlineations made by the testator, if unattested, are to be proved by the affidavits of two persons as to his handwriting. If the same are in the handwriting of any person other than the testator, it will suffice to prove by affidavit that such alterations and interlineations were known to and approved of by the testator. Proof by affidavit that they existed in the paper at the time it was found in the repositories of the testator recently after his death may, under circumstances, suffice. Alterations and interlineations made since the 31st December, 1837, are subject to the provisions of 1 Vic. c. 26.

Deeds, etc., referred to in a will or annexed to a will.

26 P.R. and 31 D.R.—With respect to deeds, papers, memoranda, or other documents mentioned in a testamentary paper, or appearing to have been annexed or attached thereto, the foregoing rules, orders and instructions as to wills, bearing date since the 31st December, 1837, will apply.

Re-publication by codicil.

27 P.R. and 32 D.R.—A will made before the 1st January, 1838, is re-published by a subsequent codicil thereto duly executed.

AS TO LETTERS OF ADMINISTRATION.

[**33 D.R.**—The duties of the District Registrar in granting letters of administration are in many respects the same as in cases of probate. In both cases he must ascertain the time and place of the deceased's death, and the value of the property to be covered by the grant, and see that the applicant has been sworn as required by statute 55 Geo. III. c. 184.]

Notice to other next-of-kin.

28 P.R. and 34 D.R.—Where administration is applied for by one or some of the next-of-kin only, there being another or other next-of-kin equally entitled thereto, the [District] Registrar may require proof by affidavit or statutory declaration that notice of such application has been given to such other next-of-kin.

Limited administrations.

29 P.R. and 35 D.R.—*Limited administrations* are not to be granted unless every person entitled to the general grant has consented or renounced, or has been cited and failed to appear, except under the direction of the Judge.

30 P.R. and 36 D.R.—No person entitled to a general grant of administration of the personal estate and effects of the deceased will be permitted to take a limited grant, except under the direction of the Judge.

Administrations under section 73.

31 P.R. and 37 D.R.—Whenever the Court, under s. 73, appoints an administrator other than the person who, prior to the Court of Probate Act, 1857, would have been entitled to the grant, the same is to be made plainly to appear in the oath of the administrator, in the letters of administration and in the administration bond.

Grants to an attorney.

32 P.R. and 38 D.R.—In the case of a person residing out of England, administration, or administration with the will annexed, may be granted to his attorney, acting under a power of attorney.

Grants of administration to guardians.

33 P.R. and 39 D.R.—Grants of administration may be made to guardians of minors and infants for their use and benefit, and elections by minors of their next-of-kin or next friend, as the case may be, will be required; but proxies accepting such guardianships and assignments of guardians to minors will be dispensed with.

34 P.R. and 40 D.R.—In all cases of infants (*i.e.*, under the age of seven years), not having a testamentary guardian or a guardian appointed by the High Court of Chancery, a guardian must be assigned by order of the Judge, or of one of the Registrars [of the Principal Registry]; the Registrar's order is to be founded on an affidavit showing that the proposed guardian is either *de facto* next-of-kin of the infants, or that their next-of-kin *de facto* has renounced his or her right to the guardianship, and is consenting to the assignment of the proposed guardian, and that such proposed guardian is ready to undertake the guardianship.

35 P.R. and 41 D.R.—Where there are both minors and infants, the guardian elected by the minors may act for the infants without being specially assigned to them, by order of the Judge or a Registrar [of the Principal Registry], provided that the object in view is to take a grant. If the object be to renounce a grant, the guardian must be specially assigned to the infants by order of the Judge or of a Registrar [of the Principal Registry].

36 P.R. and 42 D.R.—In all cases where grants of administration are to be made for the use and benefit of minors or infants, the administrators are to exhibit a declaration on oath of the personal estate and effects of the deceased, except when the effects are sworn under the value of £20, or when the administrators are the guardians appointed by the High Court of Chancery, or other competent Court, or are the testamentary guardians of the minors or infants.

Administrator's oath.

37 P.R. and 43 D.R.—The oath of administrators, and of administrators with the will, is to be so worded as to clear off all persons having a prior right to the grant, and the grant is to show on the face of it how the prior interests have been cleared off, and is to set forth, when the fact is so, that the party applying is the only next-of-kin, or one of the next-of-kin of the deceased. In all administrations of a special character, the recitals in the oath and in the letters of administration must be framed in accordance with the facts of the case.

Administration bonds.

38 P.R. and 44 D.R.—Administration bonds are to be attested by an officer of the Principal Registry, by a District Registrar or his chief clerk, or by a Commissioner or other person now or hereafter to be authorised to administer oaths under 20 and 21 Vic. c. 77, and 21 and 22 Vic. c. 95, but in no case are they to be attested by the proctor, solicitor, attorney or agent of the party who executes them. The signature of the administrator or administratrix to such bonds, if not taken in the Principal [or District] Registry, must be attested by the same person who administers the oath to such administrator or administratrix.

[**45 D.R.**—In ordinary cases two sureties are to be required, but when the property is *bonâ fide* under the value of £50, one surety only may be taken to the administration bond].

39 P.R. and 46 D.R.—In all cases of limited or special administration two sureties are to be required to the administration bond (unless the administrator be the husband of the deceased or his representative, in which case but one surety will be required), and the bond is to be given in double the amount of the property to be placed in the possession of or dealt with by the administrator by means of the grant. The alleged value of such property is to be verified by affidavit if required.

40 P.R. and 47 D.R.—The administration bond is, in all cases of limited or special administrations, to be prepared in the [District] Registry.

41 P.R. and 48 D.R.—The [District] Registrars are to take care (as far as possible) that the sureties to administration bonds are responsible persons.

Justification of sureties.

42 P.R. and 49 D.R.—When any person takes letters of administration in default of the appearance of persons cited, but not personally served with the citation, and when any person takes letters of administration for the use and benefit of a lunatic or person of unsound mind, unless he be a committee appointed by the Court of Chancery, a declaration of the personal estate and effects of the deceased must be filed in the Registry, and the sureties to the administration bond must justify.

GENERAL RULES AND ORDERS FOR THE PRINCIPAL AND DISTRICT REGISTRARS.

Last wills.

[**50 D.R.**—The District Registrar is not, in any case in which a will apparently duly executed has been produced to him for probate or for administration with the will annexed, to grant probate of any former will, or administration with any former will annexed, or administration to the deceased as having died intestate, without an order of the Judge or of one of the Registrars of the Principal Registry, showing that the last will is not entitled to probate. In the absence of such order the District Registrar is to communicate with the Registrars of the Principal Registry].

Time of issuing grant.

43 P.R. and 51 D.R.—No probate or letters of administration, with the will annexed, shall issue until after the lapse of seven days from the death of the deceased, unless under the direction of the Judge, or by order of one* of the Registrars [of the Principal Registry].

44 P.R. and 52 D.R.—No letters of administration shall issue until after the lapse of fourteen days from the death of the deceased, unless under the direction of the Judge, or by order of one* of the Registrars [of the Principal Registry].

45 P.R. and 53 D.R.—In every case where probate or administration is, for the first time, applied for after the lapse of three years from the death of the deceased, the reason of the delay is to be certified by the practitioner to the [District] Registrar. Should the certificate be unsatisfactory, [or the case be one of personal application, the District Registrar is

---

* In the Principal Registry " two."

to require an affidavit, or to communicate with the Registrars of the Principal Registry], the Registrars are to require such proof of the alleged cause of delay as they may see fit.

Filling up grants.

46 P.R. and 54 D.R.—Every grant of probate or of letters of administration issued from the [District] Registry is to be filled up there [and any former grant which has been revoked or has ceased is to be cleared off therein].

Notices of applications.

[**55 D.R.**—Notices of applications for grants of probate or administration, with the will annexed, transmitted by the District Registrar to the Registrars of the Principal Registry, are to contain (in addition to the particulars specified in s. 49 of the Court of Probate Act, 1857) an extract of the words of the will or codicil by which the applicant has been appointed executor, or of the words (if any) upon which he founds his claim to such administration].

[**56 D.R.**—Notices of application are to set forth the names and interests of all persons who, according to the practice of the Court, would have a prior right to the applicant, and to show how such prior right is cleared off. In case the persons or any of them have renounced, the date of his or her renunciation must be stated. If the applicant claims as the representative of another person, the date and particulars of the grant to him must appear].

Oaths of executors and administrators.

47 P.R. and 57 D.R.—The usual oath of administrators, as well as that of executors and administrators with the will, is to be subscribed and sworn by them as an affidavit, and then filed in the Registry.

[**58 D.R.**—The draft oaths to lead grants of special or limited probate or administration, with or without the will annexed, are to be transmitted by the District Registrar to the Registrars of the Principal Registry, in order to their being settled, and no special or limited grant is to issue until the draft oath to lead the same has been settled by a Registrar of the Principal Registry].

Identity of parties.

48 P.R. and 59 D.R.—The [District] Registrars may in cases where they deem it necessary, require proof, in addition to the oath of the executor or administrator, of the identity of the deceased, or of the party applying for the grant.

Testamentary papers to be marked.

49 P.R. and 60 D.R.—Every will, copy of a will, or other testamentary paper to which an executor or administrator with the will is sworn, must be marked by such executor or administrator and by the person before whom he is sworn.

Renunciations.

50 P.R. and 61 D.R.—No person who renounces probate of a will or letters of administration of the personal estate and effects of a deceased person in one character is to be allowed to take a representation to the same deceased in another character.

Revocation and alteration of grants.

[**62 D.R.**—Grants of probate or letters of administration can only be revoked by order of the Judge or of one of the Registrars of the Principal Registry].

[**63 D.R.**—No grant of probate or letters of administration is to be altered by a District Registrar, without an order of a Registrar of the Principal Registry having been previously obtained. In case the name of the testator or intestate requires alteration, the notice of application must be renewed, and the alteration ordered is not to be made by the District Registrar until the usual certificate on such notice has been received from the Principal Registry].

Affidavits.

51 P.R. and 64 D.R.—Every affidavit is to be drawn in the first person, and the addition and true place of abode of every deponent making it is to be inserted therein.

52 P.R. and 65 D.R.—In every affidavit made by two or more deponents, the names of the several persons making the affidavit shall be inserted in the jurat, except that, if the affidavit of all the deponents is taken at one time by the same officer, it shall be sufficient to state that it was sworn by both (or all) of the "above-named" deponents.

53 P.R. and 66 D.R.—No affidavit having in the jurat or body thereof any interlineation, alteration or erasure, shall be filed or made use of unless the interlineation or alteration, other than by erasure, is authenticated by the initials of the officer taking the affidavit, nor, in the case of any erasure, unless the words or figures appearing at the time of taking the affidavit to be written on the erasure are re-written and signed or initialled in the margin of the affidavit by the officer taking it.

54 P.R. and 67 D.R.—Where an affidavit is made by any person who is blind, or who, from his or her signature or otherwise, appears to be illiterate, the [District] Registrar, Commissioner, or other authority before whom such affidavit is made, is to state in the jurat that the affidavit was read in the presence of the person making the same, and that such person seemed perfectly to understand the same, and also made his or her mark, or wrote his or her signature, in the presence of the [District] Registrar, Commissioner, or other authority before whom the affidavit was made.

55 P.R. and 68 D.R.—No affidavit is to be deemed sufficient which has been sworn before the party on whose behalf the same is offered, or before his proctor, solicitor or attorney, or before a partner or clerk of his proctor, solicitor or attorney.

56 P.R. and 69 D.R.—Proctors, solicitors and attorneys, and their clerks respectively, if acting for any other proctor, solicitor or attorney, shall be subject to the rules in respect of taking affidavits which are applicable to those in whose stead they are acting.

57 P.R. and 70 D.R.—In every case where an affidavit is made by a subscribing witness to a will or codicil, such subscribing witness shall depose as to the mode in which the said will or codicil was executed and attested.

58 P.R. and 71 D.R.—The [District] Registrars are not to allow any affidavit to be filed [unless with the concurrence of the Registrars of the Principal Registry] which is not fairly and legibly written, or in which there is any interlineation, the extent of which at the time the affidavit was made is not clearly shown by the initials of the Commissioner or other person before whom it was sworn. *In the Principal Registry the leave of the judge must be obtained.*

Caveats.

59 P.R. and 72 D.R.—Any person intending to oppose the issuing of a grant of probate or letters of administration must, either personally or by his proctor, solicitor or attorney, enter a caveat in the Principal Registry, or in the proper District Registry. If in the Principal Registry the person entering the caveat must also insert the name of the deceased in the Index to the Caveat Book.

60 P.R. and 73 D.R.—A caveat shall bear date on the day it is entered, and shall remain in force for the space of six months only, and then expire and be of no effect; but caveats may be renewed from time to time.

61 P.R. and 74 D.R.—The [District] Registrar shall, immediately upon a caveat being entered, send a copy thereof [to the Registrars of the Principal Registry, and also] to the Registrar of any [other] District in which it is alleged the deceased resided at the time of his death, or in which he is known to have had a fixed place of abode at the time of his death.

62 P.R. and 75 D.R.—No caveat shall affect any grant made on the day on which the caveat is entered, *or on the day on which notice is received* of a caveat having been entered in the District [*or* Principal] Registry.

63 P.R.—All caveats shall be warned from the Principal Registry only. The warning is to be left at the place mentioned in the caveat as the address of the person who entered it.

64 P.R.—It shall be sufficient for the warning of a caveat that a Registrar send by the public post a warning signed by himself, and directed to the person who entered the caveat, at the address mentioned in it.

65 P.R.—The warning to a caveat is to state the name and interest of the party on whose behalf the same is issued, and if such person claims under a will or codicil, is also to state the date of such will or codicil, and is to contain an address within three miles of the General Post Office, at which any notice requiring service may be left. The form of warning will be supplied in the Registry.

66 P.R.—Before any citation is signed by a Registrar, a caveat shall be entered against any grant being made in respect of the estate and effects of the deceased to which such citation relates, and notice thereof shall be sent to the District Registrar of any District in which the deceased appears to have resided at the time of his death.

67 P.R.—In order to clear off a caveat when no appearance has been entered to a warning duly served, an affidavit of the service of the warning, stating the manner of service and an affidavit of search for appearance and of non-appearance, must be filed.

[**76 D.R.**—Caveats shall be warned from the Principal Registry only].

[**77 D.R.**—After a caveat has been entered, the District Registrar is not to proceed with the grant of probate or administration to which it relates until it has expired or been subducted, or until he has received notice from the Principal Registry that the caveat has been warned and no appearance given, or that the contentious proceedings consequent on the caveat have terminated].

[**78 D.R.**—The further rules in respect to caveats will be found in the " Rules, Orders, and Instructions for the Registrars of the Principal Registry "].

Citations and subpœnas.

68 P.R.—No citation is to issue under seal of the Court until an affidavit, in verification of the averments it contains, has been filed in the Registry.

69 P.R.—Citations are to be served personally when that can be done. Personal service shall be effected by leaving a true copy of the citation with the party cited, and showing him the original, if required by him so to do.

70 P.R.—Citations and other instruments which cannot be personally served are to be served by the insertion of the same, or of an abstract thereof, settled and signed by one of the Registrars as an advertisement in such morning and evening London newspapers, and such local newspapers, and at such intervals as the Judge or one of the Registrars may direct.

[**79 D.R.**—Citations and subpœnas can be issued from the Principal Registry only, and the rules applicable to them will be found in the " Rules, Orders, and Instructions for the Registrars of the Principal Registry "].

[**80 D.R.**—No grants are to issue from a District Registry after a citation without the production of an office copy of the decree or order of the Judge, or of one of the Registrars of the Principal Registry authorising the same].

Blind and illiterate testators.

71 P.R. or 81 D.R.—The [District] Registrars are not to allow probate of the will, or administration with the will annexed, of any blind or obviously illiterate or ignorant person, to issue, unless they have previously satisfied themselves that the said will was read over to the testator before its execution, or that the testator had at such time knowledge of its contents.   [When such information is not forthcoming, the District Registrars are to communicate with the Registrars of the Principal Registry].

Alterations in grants, etc.

72 P.R.—When any alteration is made in a Grant of Probate or Letters of Administration which has issued from a District Probate Registry, or when any such a Grant is revoked and the Volume of the printed Calendar containing the entry of the Grant has been forwarded to the District Registrars, Notice of such alteration or revocation is without delay to be forwarded by the Registrars of the Principal Registry to the District Probate Registrar from whose Registry the altered or revoked Grant issued.

[82 **D.R.**—Whenever the value of the personal estate and effects of a deceased person is resworn under a different amount, or any alteration is made in a grant, or a renunciation is filed, notice of such reswearing, alteration or renunciation is without delay to be forwarded by the District Registrar to the Registrars of the Principal Registry, but no fee shall be payable in respect of any such notice].

Lists of grants.

[83 **D.R.**—The lists of grants of probate and administration required to be furnished by the District Registrars under s. 51 of the Court of Probate Act, 1857, are to be furnished on the first and every other Thursday in the month, and are to contain the name of the Registry in which each grant was made, and the Christian and surname of each testator and intestate].

[84 **D.R.**—Every such list of grants furnished by the District Registrar is to be accompanied by a copy of the record of each grant mentioned in it. The record, besides stating the necessary particulars of the grant to which it refers, is to contain the place and time of death of the testator or intestate; the names and description of each executor or administrator; the date of each grant; and the sum under which the value of the personal estate and effects is sworn, and in cases of administrations the names and description of the sureties].

[85 **D.R.**—Within four days from the end of each month each District Registrar is to forward to the Principal Registry

M

a return, arranged alphabetically, of all grants of probate or letters of administration passed at his District Registry during the preceding month].

Irish Grants.

73 P.R.—The Seal is not to be affixed to any probate or letters of administration granted in Ireland, so as to give operation thereto as if the grant had been made by the Court of Probate in England, unless it appear from a Certificate of the Commissioners of Inland Revenue, or their proper officer, that such probate or letters of administration is duly stamped in respect of the personal estate and effects of which the deceased died possessed in England. In respect to letters of administration, the provisions of statute 21 & 22 Vict. c. 95, s. 29, must also be complied with.

Grants for property in the United Kingdom, etc.

74 P.R. and 86 D.R.—Whenever a grant of probate or of letters of administration is made under Statute 21 & 22 Vic. c. 56, for the whole personal estate and effects of a deceased within the United Kingdom, it must appear by the affidavit made for the Inland Revenue Office that the testator, or intestate, died domiciled in England, and that he was possessed of personal estate in Scotland other than that excluded by 22 & 23 Vic. c. 80, and the value of such personal estate must be separately stated in such affidavit. In case any portion of the personal estate be in Ireland, a separate affidavit and schedule must also be filed. Upon all such grants a note or memorandum must also be written and signed by the [District] Registrar to the effect that the testator or intestate died domiciled in England.

[**87 D.R.**—Grants of probate and administration made in Ireland, and confirmations granted in Scotland, must be taken to the Principal Registry, and not to a District Registry, to be sealed with the seal of the Court of Probate, in order to the same having force and effect in England].

Notices to Queen's Proctor.

75 P.R. and 88 D.R.—In all cases where application is made for letters of administration (with or without a will annexed) of the goods of a bastard dying a bachelor or a spinster, or a widower or widow without issue, notice of such application is to be given to Her Majesty's Procurator-General (or in case the deceased died domiciled within the Duchy of Lancaster, to the Solicitor for the Duchy in London), in order that he may determine whether he will interfere on the part of the Crown; and no grant is to be issued until the officer of the Crown has signified the course which he thinks proper to take.

76 P.R.—In the case of persons dying intestate without any known relation, a citation must be issued against the next-of-kin, if any, and all persons having or pretending to have any interest in the personal estate of the deceased, and the service thereof upon them shall be effected as required by Rule 70. Such citation must also be served upon the Queen's Proctor, or upon the solicitor for the Duchy of Lancaster, as the case may require.

[**89 D.R.**—In the case of persons dying intestate without any known relation, a citation must be issued from the Principal Registry against the next-of-kin, if any, and all persons having or pretending to have any interest in the personal estate of the deceased. See the rules, orders, and instructions for the Registrars of the Principal Registry].

Transmission of Papers.

77 P.R.—After motions have been made before the judge in Court, the Registrars are, on the application of the parties (unless the judge shall otherwise direct), to transmit

M 2

to a District Registrar the original papers and documents, in order that the grant of probate or administration may be completed in a District Registry.

78 P.R.—Papers and other documents may be transmitted by the Registrars of the Principal Registry to the District Registrars through the Post Office. Such letters or packets are to be superscribed with the words, " On Her Majesty's Service," and may be registered if thought necessary.

[**90 D.R.**—When motions are to be made before the Judge in Court, with regard to any application for probate or administration at a District Registry the District Registrar is to transmit all original papers and documents to the Principal Registry, and the same, after the directions of the Court have been taken, will, on the application of the parties, be returned to the District Registrar, together with an office copy of the decree of the Judge].

[**91 D.R.**—Original papers are also to be forwarded to the Principal Registry whenever an inspection of them is necessary, in order to enable the Registrars to answer the questions submitted to them by the District Registrar].

[**92 D.R.**—Original papers and documents may be transmitted by the District Registrars to the Registrars of the Principal Registry through the Post Office. Such letters or packets are to be superscribed with the words "On Her Majesty's Service," and may be registered, if thought necessary].

Probate copies of wills.

79 P.R.—The Registrars are to take care that the copies of wills and affidavits to be annexed to the probates or letters of administration are fairly and properly written, and are to reject those which are otherwise ; but it shall not be necessary that such copies be written in the engrossing hand heretofore in use.

[**93 D.R.**—The District Registrar is to take care that the copies of wills and affidavits to be annexed to the probate or letters of administration are fairly and properly written, and is to reject those which are otherwise].

Office copies.

80 P.R. and 94 D.R.—Office copies of wills, and other documents furnished in a [District] Registry, will not be collated with the original will or other document, unless specially required. Every copy so required to be examined shall be certified under the hand of the [District] Registrar to be an examined copy.

81 P.R. and 95 D.R.—The seal of the Court is not to be affixed to any office copy of a will, or other document, unless the same has been certified to be an examined copy.

Attendances with documents.

82 P.R. and 96 D.R.—If a will or other document filed in a District Registry is required to be produced at any place within three miles of that Registry, application must be made for that purpose not later than the day previously to that named for its production.

83 P.R.—If a will or other document filed in the Registry is required to be produced at any place beyond the above distance, application must be made for that purpose in sufficient time to allow for making and examining a copy of such will or other document to be deposited in its place, and in every case such notice must be given (except by special leave of the Judge or Registrars) at least 24 hours before the clerk in whose charge the will or other document is to be placed will be required to set off.

[97 D.R.—If a will or other document filed in a District Registry is required to be produced at any place beyond the above distance, application must be made for that purpose in sufficient time to allow for making and examining a copy of such will or other document to be deposited in its place].

Doubtful and difficult cases.

[98 D.R.—The District Registrars are in every case of doubt or difficulty to communicate with the Registrars of the Principal Registry].

Subpœnas to bring in Testamentary Papers.

84 P.R.—Any person bringing in a will or testamentary paper, in obedience to a subpœna, is to take it in the first instance to the clerk of the papers, who will prepare a minute to be signed by the Registrar to whom the will or paper brought in is to be delivered, and the Registrar will sign the minute recording the delivery thereof.

85 P.R.—The minute is to be entered in the book of Registrar's Minutes in the usual manner; and the fee for the entry, and a further fee for filing each testamentary paper, will then be payable. If these fees should not be paid by the person bringing in the will or paper, the same are to be charged to the person who may first apply to the clerk of the papers to make use of the will or paper so brought in. In case the person bringing in a will or testamentary paper may desire to have a voucher for its delivery into the Registry, he may take an office copy of the minute on paying the usual fee for the same.

86 P.R.—Any person served with a subpœna to bring in a testamentary paper is at liberty to enter an appearance on payment of the usual fees, if he thinks fit to do so.

Time allowed for appearing to a Warning, Citation, or Subpœna.

87 P.R.—The time fixed by a warning or citation for entering an appearance, or by a subpœna, to bring in a testamentary paper, shall, in all cases, be exclusive of Sundays, Christmas Day and Good Friday.

Taxing bills of costs.

88 P.R. and 99 D.R.—All bills of costs are to be referred to the Registrars of the Principal Registry for taxation, and no special order shall be required for that purpose.

[**100 D.R.**—The rules in respect to taxing bills of costs will be found in the " Rules, Orders, and Instructions for the Registrars of the Principal Registry]."

89 P.R.—The bill of costs of any proctor, solicitor, or attorney will be taxed on his application, after sufficient notice given to the person or persons liable for the payment thereof, or on the application of such person or persons, after sufficient notice given to the practitioner, and the Registrar shall decide in each case what may be a sufficient notice.

90 P.R.—When an appointment has been made by a Registrar to tax a bill, the Registrar may proceed to tax the same after the expiration of a quarter-of-an-hour, notwithstanding the absence of either party, or his agent, provided he be satisfied that the absent party has had due notice of the appointment for taxation.

91 P.R.—If more than one-sixth is deducted from any bill of costs taxed as between practitioner and client, no costs incurred in the taxation thereof shall be allowed as part of such bill.

The following Precedents are extracted from "Guide to Preparation of Bills of Costs," by C. W. Scott.

COSTS OF PROBATES.

PRECEDENT No 1.

In the High Court of Justice.

PROBATE, DIVORCE AND ADMIRALTY DIVISION.
(PROBATE.)

In the goods of   Deceased.

	Effects sworn under £100.	Effects sworn under £200.	Effects sworn above £200 and under £1,000.
Perusing will and taking instructions for probate	£0 6 8	£0 6 8	£0 6 8
Copy will for use . . .	4d. per folio of 72 words in all cases.		
Oath of executors, and attendance on the party being sworn . .	0 5 0	0 6 8	0 10 0
Paid commissioner's fee . . .	1s. 6d. each deponent and 1s. each exhibit.		
Affidavit of value and inventory for Inland Revenue, and attendance on the party being sworn charge according to circumstances for time and trouble in getting necessary information, and for affidavit, at per folio	0 1 4	0 1 4	0 1 4
Paid commissioner's fee . . .	1s. 6d. each deponent.		
Engrossing and collating the will, 3 folios of 90 words or under, including parchment . . .	0 4 6	0 4 6	0 4 6
If exceeding 3 folios of 90 words, then every other folio	0 1 6	0 1 6	0 1 6
Stamp on receipt . . .	0 1 0	0 1 0	0 1 0
Paid Probate [*or* Estate] duty .	Nil.	*	*
Stamp fee on search . . .	6d. for every year after the death.		
Probate under seal (solicitor's fees) .	0 1 0	0 3 0	†

  ° For the duty on Probates, *see* Chapter 3.

  † For amounts to be inserted opposite "Probate under seal" and "Court fees," *see* next page.

	Effects sworn under £100.			Effects sworn under £200.			Effects sworn above £200 and under £1,000.		
Extracting	£0	6	8	£0	6	8	£0	6	8
Clerk's fee	0	2	0	0	2	0	0	2	0
Paid Court fees									
Registering and collating will, 3 folios of 90 words or under . .	0	4	6	0	4	6	0	4	6
If exceeding 3 folios of 90 words then at per folio . . .	0	1	6	0	1	6	0	1	6
Registrar's certificate . . .	0	2	6	0	2	6	0	2	6
Letters, messengers, etc. . .	0	5	0	0	5	0	0	10	0

The amounts to be inserted opposite "Probate under seal" and "Court fees" are as follows :—

			Probate under seal.					
			Solicitor's fees.			Court fees.		
If effects sworn under £300			£0	7	6	£0	7	6
,, ,, 450			0	12	0	0	12	0
,, ,, 600			0	16	6	0	16	6
,, ,, 800			1	2	6	1	2	6
,, ,, 1,000			1	13	0	1	13	0

NOTE.—By Section 33 of the Act, 44 Vic., chap. 12, where the *gross* estate is under £300, the Court fee is 15s. only; and by Section 16 of the Act, 57 & 58 Vic., chap. 30, where the *gross* estate is under £500, the Court fee is 15s. only.

Where the property is sworn at an exact sum such as £1,000 or £10,000, the Probate Duty or Estate Duty is charged on those sums, but the Court fee is charged on the next highest amount.

PRECEDENT No. 2.

	Effects sworn under £2,000.	Effects sworn under £1,000.	Effects sworn above £1,000 and under £70,000.
Perusing will and taking instructions for Probate . . .	£0 13 4	£0 13 4	£1 1 0
Or according to circumstances.			
Copy will for use . . .	4d. per folio of 72 words in all cases.		
Oath of executor and attendance on the party being sworn . .	£0 10 0	£0 10 0	£0 10 0
Paid commissioner's fee . .	1s. 6d. each deponent and 1s. each exhibit.		
Affidavit of value and inventory for Inland Revenue and attendance on the party being sworn (*charge for affidavit at per folio 1s. 4d. and for extra trouble and attendances in getting necessary information according to circumstances.*)			
Paid commissioner's fee . .	1s. 6d. each deponent.		
Engrossing and collating the will, 3 folios of 90 words or under, including parchment . .	0 4 6	0 4 6	0 4 6
If exceeding 3 folios of 90 words then . . .	1s. 6d. for every other folio.		
Stamp on receipt . . .	0 1 0	0 1 0	0 1 0
Paid Probate [*or Estate*] duty .	*	*	*
Stamp fee on search . . .	6d. for every year after the death.		
Probate under seal (solicitor's fees) .	†	†	†
Extracting	0 6 8	0 13 4	0 13 4
Clerk's fee	0 5 0	0 5 0	0 7 6
Paid Court fees . . .	†	†	†
Registering and collating will, 3 folios of 90 words or under .	0 4 6	0 4 6	0 4 6
If exceeding 3 folios then at per folio . . .	0 1 6	0 1 6	0 1 6
Registrar's certificate . .	0 2 6	0 2 6	0 2 6
Letters, messengers, etc. . .	0 10 0	0 10 0	0 13 4
Or more according to circumstances.			

* For duty on Probates, *see* Chapter 3.

† The fees to be inserted at "Probate under seal" and "Court fees" are identical; they will be found at page 118.

For example :—

	Solicitor's fee.	Court fee.
Under £1,500 .	£2 5 0	£2 5 0
„ 1,600 .	3 0 0	3 0 0
„ 2,000 .	3 0 0	3 0 0
„ 2,100 .	3 15 0	3 15 0
„ 3,000 .	3 15 0	3 15 0
„ 3,100 .	4 10 0	4 10 0

PRECEDENT No. 3.

Effects sworn above £70,000 and under £500,000.

Instructions for Probate £2 2 0
          Or according to circumstances.
Copy will for use . . . 4d. per folio of 72 words in all cases.
Oath of executors and attendance on the party being sworn . 0 10 0
Paid commissioner's fee . 1s. 6d. each deponent, and 1s. each exhibit.
Affidavit of value and inventory for Inland Revenue and
    attendance on the party being sworn (*charge according to
    circumstances for time and trouble in getting necessary
    information and for Affidavit at per folio 1s. 4d.*)
Paid commissioner's fee . . . . . 1s. 6d. each deponent.
Engrossing and collating the will, 3 folios of 90. words or
    under, including parchment 0 4 6
    If exceeding 3 folios of 90 words, then . 1s. 6d. for every other folio.
Stamp on receipt 0 1 0
Paid Probate [*or Estate*] duty . . . .
Stamp fee on search . . . . 6d. per year in all cases.
Probate under seal (solicitor's fee) . . . . *
Extracting 0 13 4
Clerk's fee 1 1 0
Paid court fees . . . . *
Registering and collating will, 3 folios of 90 words or under . 0 4 6
    If exceeding 3 folios then for each folio . . . 0 1 6
Registrar's certificate 0 2 6
Letters, messengers, etc. 1 1 0
          Or according to circumstances.

* The amounts to be inserted opposite " Probate under seal" and
" Court fees" are as follows :—

		Probate under seal. Solicitor's fees.			Probate under seal. Court fees.		
If effects sworn under £80,000		£16	17	6	£16	17	6
„	„ 90,000	18	15	0	18	15	0
„	„ 100,000	20	12	6	20	12	6
„	„ 120,000	21	11	3	21	11	3
„	„ 140,000	23	8	9	23	8	9
„	„ 160,000	25	6	3	25	6	3
„	„ 180,000	27	3	9	27	3	9
„	„ 200,000	29	1	3	29	1	3
„	„ 250,000	30	18	9	30	18	9
„	„ 300,000	35	12	6	35	12	6
„	„ 350,000	40	6	3	40	6	3
„	„ 400,000	41	17	6	41	17	6
„	„ 500,000	43	8	9	43	8	9

Additional charges where necessary.

And for every additional £100,000, or any fractional part of £100,000, under which the personal estate is sworn, in addition to the above fees, a further fee for probate under seal of £3 2 6

In addition to the above for all second or subsequent grants of probate or letters of administration with will annexed, the same fees for looking up the will and bespeaking engrossment as on similar grants upon which no stamp duty is payable.

When there are two or more executors, and they are not sworn at the same time, for each attendance after the first on their being sworn to oath and affidavit—

If the effects are sworn under £20 . . . . . 0 2 6
If the effects are sworn under £100 . . . . . 0 5 0
If the effects are sworn above £100 . . . . . 0 6 8

In respect of Letters of Administration with Will annexed.

In addition to the above fees for preparing and attendance on the execution of the bond if the effects are—

Under £20 . . . . 0 2 6
£20 and under £100 . . . . 0 6 8
£100 and upwards 0 10 0

Paid commissioner 1s. 6d. and court fee stamp 5s.

For engrossing and collating a will or codicil for a grant of probate or letters of administration with the will annexed, when there are pencil marks in the will or codicil, or when the will or codicil is to be registered fac-simile, in addition to any other fee for engrossing and collating the same—

If the pencil marks in the will or codicil, or the part or parts thereof to be registered fac-simile, are two folios of ninety words in length or under 0 1 0
If exceeding two folios, for every additional folio or part of folio of ninety words 0 0 6

COSTS OF ADMINISTRATIONS.

PRECEDENT No. 4.

In the High Court of Justice.

PROBATE, DIVORCE AND ADMIRALTY DIVISION,
(PROBATE.)

In the goods of

Deceased.

	Effects sworn under £100.			Effects sworn under £200.			Effects sworn above £200 and under £800.		
Instructions for administration . .	£0	3	4	£0	6	8	£0	6	8
Oath of administrator, and attendance on his being sworn, and on his execution of the bond . .	0	6	8	0	10	0	0	13	4
Commissioner's fee	1s. 6d. each deponent and 1s. 6d. on each execution of bond.								
Affidavit of value and inventory for Inland Revenue and attending administrator on his being sworn (*Charge for affidavit per folio 1s. 4d. and according to circumstances for time and trouble in getting necessary information.*)									
Commissioner's fee	1s. 6d. each deponent.								
Instructions for bond . . .	0	6	8	0	6	8	0	6	8
Drawing and engrossing same .	0	5	0	0	6	8	0	6	8
Paid stamp on bond . . .	Nil			0	5	0	0	5	0
Attending sureties on their reading over, and with them on their executing bond	0	6	8	0	6	8	0	6	8
Commissioner's fee	1s. 6d. each surety.								
Stamp on receipt	0	1	0	0	1	0	0	1	0
The Registrar having required a certificate of cause of delay in taking out the grant. Drawing same	0	5	0	0	5	0	0	5	0
Paid fee on filing . . .	0	2	6	0	2	6	0	2	6

	Effects sworn under £100.	Effects sworn under £200.	Effects sworn above £200 and under £800.
Registrar's certificate . . .	£0 2 6	£0 2 6	£0 2 6
Paid Probate [or Estate] duty .	Nil		
(*The duty on administrations is the same as on probates, and will be found in Chapter 3.*) .			
Stamp fee on search . . .	6d. for every year after death.		
Letters of administration under seal	0 3 0	0 4 6	*
Extracting	0 6 8	0 6 8	0 6 8
Clerks	0 2 0	0 2 0	0 2 0
Paid court fees	0 1 0	0 4 6	*
Letters, messengers, etc. . .	0 5 0	0 5 0	0 5 0
	Or according to circumstances.		

* The amount to be inserted opposite " Letters of administration under seal " and " Court fees " are as follows :—

	Letters of Administration under seal. Solicitor's fees.	Letters of Administration under seal. Court fees.
If effects sworn under £300 .	£0 12 0	£0 12 0
,, ,, 450 .	0 16 6	0 16 6
,, ,, 600 .	1 2 6	1 2 6
,, ,, 800 .	1 13 0	1 13 0

PRECEDENT No. 5.

	Effects sworn above £800 and under £1,500.	Effects sworn under £2,000.	Effects sworn above £2,000 and under £70,000.
Instructions for administration .	£0 6 8	£0 6 8	£0 13 4
Oath of administrator and attendance on his being sworn and on his execution of the bond . .	0 13 4	0 13 4	0 13 4
Commissioner's fee . . .	1s. 6d. each deponent, and 1s. 6d. on each execution of bond.		
Affidavit of value and inventory for Inland Revenue, and attending administrator on his being sworn (*Charge for affidavit per folio 1s. 4d. and according to circumstances for time and trouble in getting necessary information.*)			
Commissioner's fee .	1s. 6d. each deponent.		

	Effects sworn above £800 and under £1,500.			Effects sworn under £2,000.			Effects sworn above £2,000 and under £70,000.		
Instructions for bond . . .	£0	6	8	£0	6	8	£0	6	8
Drawing and engrossing same .	0	6	8	0	6	8	0	6	8
Paid stamp on bond . . .	0	5	0	0	5	0	0	5	0
Attending sureties on their reading over, and with them on their executing bond	0	6	8	0	6	8	0	6	8
Commissioner's fee				*1s. 6d.* each surety.					
Stamp on receipt . . .	0	1	0	0	1	0	0	1	0
The Registrar having required a certificate of cause of delay in taking out the grant. Drawing same	0	5	0	0	5	0	0	5	0
Engrossing at per folio . . .	0	0	4	0	0	4	0	0	4
Filing	0	2	6	0	2	6	0	2	6
Registrar's certificate . . .	0	2	6	0	2	6	0	2	6
Paid Probate [*or* Estate] duty . *									
Stamp fee on search . . .				*6d.* for every year after death.					
Letters of administration under seal †				4	10	0			
Extracting	0	6	8	0	13	4	0	13	4
Clerks	0	5	0	0	5	0	0	7	6
Paid Court fees— . . . †									
Letters, messengers, etc. . .	0	5	0	0	10	0	0	13	4
				Or according to circumstances.					

* For duty, *see* Chapter 3.

† The amount to be inserted opposite " Letters of administration under seal " and " Court fees " are as follows :—

					Letters of administration under seal.					
					Solicitor's fees.			Court fees.		
If effects sworn under	£850	.	.							
,,	,,	900	.	.	2	5	0	2	5	0
,,	,,	950	.	.						
,,	,,	1,000	.	.						
,,	,,	1,100	.	.						
,,	,,	1,200	.	.						
,,	,,	1,300	.	.	3	7	6	3	7	6
,,	,,	1,400	.	.						
,,	,,	1,500	.	.						

And so on, *see* page 118.

LIST OF DISTRICT REGISTRIES.

Name of Registry.	Description of District.	Date of earliest Record.	Registrars.	Chief Clerk.
BANGOR	Counties of Carnarvon and Anglesea	1635	H. B. Roberts	J. R. Williams.
BIRMINGHAM	County of Warwick, including the City of Coventry	1675	Wm. G. Middleton	Geo. Rabnett.
BLANDFORD	County of Dorset, including the Town of Poole	1568	E. A. Smith	H. J. Coward.
BODMIN	County of Cornwall	1601	W. F. L. Standwell	N. J. Pinch.
BRISTOL	Bristol and Bath, present County Court Districts	1568	W. H. Clarke	A. P. Cornish.
BURY ST. EDMUNDS	Western Division of the County of Suffolk	1354	C. Wodehouse	W. Goodchild.
CANTERBURY	East Division of the County of Kent, including the City of Canterbury, and such of the Cinque Ports and their Dependencies as are locally situate in the County of Kent	1396	H. M. Chapman	J. Browne.
CARLISLE	Counties of Cumberland and Westmoreland	1564	W. C. Butler	T. Bulman.
CARMARTHEN	Counties of Cardigan, Carmarthen, including the Town of Carmarthen, and Pembroke, including the Town of Haverfordwest, with the Deaneries of East and West Gower, in the County of Glamorgan	1600	W. M. Griffiths	H. Ll. Williams.
CHESTER	The County and City of Chester	1545	G. Middleton	C. Edwards.
CHICHESTER	Western Division of the County of Sussex	1511	Sir R. G. Raper, Knt.	H. Heather.
DERBY	County of Derby	1888	C. T. E. Wilde	J. Yates.
DURHAM	County of Durham	1540	J. Earles	A. E. Davis.
EXETER	County of Devon, including the City of Exeter	1545	W. H. Bailey	J. C. Greenslade.
GLOUCESTER	County and City of Gloucester, except the present Bristol County Court District	1541	R. Fuller	F. E. Wallis.
HEREFORD	Counties of Radnor, Brecknock and Hereford	1545	T. C. Paris	W. Earle.
IPSWICH	Eastern Division of the County of Suffolk, and North Division of the County of Essex	1444	B. P. Grimsey	G. W. Hubbard.
LANCASTER	County of Lancaster, except the Hundred of Salford and West Derby and the City of Manchester	1748	John Douglas-Willan	W. H. Winder.
LEICESTER	Counties of Leicester and Rutland	1500	G. H. Nevinson	F. T. Jackson.
LEWES	Eastern Division of the County of Sussex, including such of the Cinque Ports and their Dependencies as are locally situate in the County of Sussex	1541	J. W. Heisch	W. G. Foster.

LIST OF DISTRICT REGISTRIES—*continued.*

Name of Registry.	Description of District.	Date of earliest Record.	Registrar.	Chief Clerk.
LICHFIELD	County of Stafford, including the City of Lichfield	1526	T. W. H. Oakley	W. Austin.
LINCOLN	County and City of Lincoln	1506	J. Swan	B. Robinson.
LIVERPOOL	Hundred of West Derby in Lancashire	1858	T. E. Paget	H. Lewis.
LLANDAFF	Counties of Glamorgan (with the exception of the Deaneries of East and West Gower) and Monmouth	1590	C. Waldron	T. C. Thomas,
MANCHESTER	City of Manchester and Hundred of Salford	1658	O. H. Hardy	H. J. Cutter.
NEWCASTLE-UPON-TYNE	County of Northumberland, including the Towns and Counties of Newcastle-upon-Tyne and Berwick-upon-Tweed	1658	H. Exley Edwards	F. W. Bell.
NORTHAMPTON	The Town of Northampton, County of Bedford and Southern Division of Northamptonshire	1496	C. C. Becke	H. W. Groves.
NORWICH	County of Norfolk, including the City of Norwich	1370	G. R. Harman	B. R. G. Watling.
NOTTINGHAM	County and City of Nottingham	1658	W. G. Vincent	J. A. Price.
OXFORD	Counties of Oxford (including the University), Berks and Buckingham	1801	T. M. Davenport	G. W. Barker.
PETERBOROUGH	Northern Division of Northampton and Counties of Huntingdon and Cambridge, including the University of Cambridge	1603	H. W. Gates	W. H. Jamblin.
ST. ASAPH	Counties of Flint, Denbigh and Merioneth	1565	J. P. Lewis	R. Jones.
SALISBURY	County of Wilts	1900	H. Elliott Fox	H. Young.
SHREWSBURY	Counties of Salop and Montgomery	1635	F. R. B. Walton	Bryce Smith.
TAUNTON	Western Division of the County of Somerset	1538	E. T. Alms	W. J. Jewell.
WAKEFIELD	West Riding of the County of York	1587	G. Bridgeman	B. Wales.
WELLS	Eastern Division of the County of Somerset, except the present Bath County Court District and the part in Somersetshire of the present Bristol County Court District			
WINCHESTER	County of Hants, including the Town of Southampton and Isle of Wight	1530	L. Ellicott	T. L. Gleaves.
WORCESTER	City and County of Worcester	1398	C. Woolbridge	W. C. Gaiger.
YORK	North and East Ridings of the County of York, including the City of York and Ainsty, and the Town and County of Kingston-upon-Hull	1493	H. A. Franklin	T. Wilson.
		1398	H. A. Hudson	E. C. Birks.

N.B.—The expression "the present," where used in the foregoing description, refers to August, 1857.

N

TABLE OF SUCCESSION TO REAL AND PERSONAL PROPERTY.

Under 3 & 4 Wm. IV., c. 106; 22 & 23 Car. II., c. 10; 29 Car. II., c. 30; and 1 Jac. II., c. 17

Customs of London and York and other places are now abolished, so far as they affect *personal* property of persons dying after 31st Dec., 1856 (19 & 20 Vic., c. 94); but the customs of Gavelkind and Borough English still affect *real* property in certain localities, the former principally in Kent.

The following is a short Table showing how Property is distributed in cases where the owner dies entitled in his own right, without having made a will or settlement; the fourth column also shows what persons would be entitled to letters of administration entitling them to the right of receiving and distributing the personal estate.

N.B.—In each instance it is supposed there are no nearer relations than those named.

If a Person die leaving	LAND.—Real Property (except leaseholds) would descend	MONEY.—Personal Property (including leaseholds) would be divided	Persons entitled to administration.
*Widow and no relations	One-third to widow for life, rest to the Crown (copyholds to the Lord of the Manor) (*Note A. & D.*)	Half to widow, rest to the Crown	Widow.
*Widow and father	One-third to widow for life, rest to father if the deceased had acquired the fee by purchase and not by descent (*Note A.*)	Equally	Widow.
*Widow and mother	One-third to widow for life, rest to mother in default of any heirs on father's side (*Note A.*)	Equally (*Keilway* v. *Keilway,* 2 *P. Wms.,* 344)	Widow.
*Widow, father, brothers, and sisters	One-third to widow for life, rest to father if the deceased had acquired the fee by purchase and not by descent (*Note A.*)	Equally between widow and father	Widow.
*Widow, mother, brothers, and sisters, whether by whole or half-blood	One-third to widow for life, rest to eldest brother (by whole blood) (*Note A.*)	Half to widow, rest equally divided between mother, brothers and sisters	Widow.
*Widow, mother, nephews, and nieces (children of deceased brother)	One-third to widow for life, rest to nephew (eldest son of brother) or nieces (daughters of deceased brother if he left no son) (*Note A.*)	Half to widow, one-fourth to mother, rest between nephews and nieces (*Stanley* v. *Stanley,* 1 *Atk.*)	Widow.
*Widow, brothers, and sisters	One-third to widow for life, rest to eldest brother (*Note A.*)	Half to widow, rest equally to brothers and sisters	Widow.
Widow, sons, and daughters (*Note C.*)	One-third to widow for life, rest to eldest son (*Note A.*)	One-third to widow, rest equally amongst sons and daughters	Widow.
Widow and daughter (*Note C.*)	One-third to widow for life, rest to daughter (*Note A.*)	One-third to widow, rest to daughter	Widow.
Widow and daughters (*Note C.*)	One-third to widow for life, rest equally between daughters (*Note A.*)	One-third to widow, rest equally between daughters	Widow.

Note: "Subject to payment of the £500 to the widow under the Intestate's Act, 1890, as to which see note at foot." and "Subject to payment of the £500 to the widow, as aforesaid."

* By the Intestate's Estates Act, 1890, the real and personal property of a man who dies after 1st September 1890, leaving a widow but no issue, shall, where the value of such property is less than £500, belong to the widow absolutely, and where the value exceeds £500 she shall be entitled to £500 part thereof absolutely and in addition to her share of the residue, as if such residue had been the whole estate before the passing of this Act, such sum to be paid out of the realty and personalty rateably.

If a Person die leaving	LAND.—Real Property (except leaseholds) would descend	MONEY.—Personal Property (including leaseholds) would be divided	Persons entitled to administration.
Widow and grandchildren (sons of deceased son)	One-third to widow for life, rest to eldest son of eldest deceased son (Note A.)	One-third to widow, rest equally between grandchildren	Widow.
Husband (where there has been issue born alive capable of inheriting the realty)	All for life, afterwards to heir at law (Note B.)	All (Note E.)	Husband.
Husband (where there has not been issue born alive capable of inheriting the realty)	To heir at law	All to husband (Note E.)	Husband.
Husband, sons and daughters	All to husband for life, afterwards to eldest son (Note B.)	All to husband (Note E.)	Husband.
Husband and child (son or daughter)	All to husband for life, afterwards to child (Note B.)	All to husband (Note E.)	Husband.
Husband and daughters	All to husband for life, afterwards to daughters equally (Note B.)	All to husband (Note E.)	Husband.
Husband and grandchildren (daughters of deceased son or daughter)	All to husband for life, afterwards to grandchildren equally (Note B.)	All to husband (Note E.)	Husband.
Sons and daughters, whether by one or more wife or wives, and whether or not posthumous	All to eldest son	Equally divided (*Wallis v. Hodson*, 2 Atk., 117)	Either son or daughter, or any number not exceeding three of either or both.
One child, either son or daughter	All	All	Child.
Daughters	Equally divided	Equally divided	Either or any number of them not exceeding three.
(Eldest) son and grandchild (son or daughter of younger son)	All to eldest son	Equally divided	Eldest son.
(Younger) son and grandchild (son or daughter of eldest son)	All to grandchild	Equally divided	Younger son.
Eldest son, sons and daughters, and grandchildren	All to eldest son	Equally divided (but grandchildren only take deceased parent's share equally between them)	To any son or daughter, or any number not exceeding three of either or both.
Daughters and grandchild (son or daughter of deceased son)	All to grandchild	Equally	To any daughter, or any number of them not exceeding three.
Daughters and grandchildren (children of deceased son)	All to granddaughters	Equally (but granddaughters only take their father's share between them)	To any daughter, or any number of them not exceeding three.

If a Person die leaving	LAND.—Real Property (except leaseholds) would descend	MONEY.—Personal Property (including leaseholds) would be divided	Persons entitled to administration.
Daughters and grandchildren (sons and daughters of deceased daughter)	Equally between daughters and eldest son of deceased daughter	Equally (but grandchildren only take their parent's share equally between them)	To any daughter, or any number of them not exceeding three.
Grandchildren (sons and daughters of two sons and daughter)	All to grandson, eldest son of eldest son	Equally *per stirpes, i.e.,* their deceased parent's share (*Re Natt. Walker v. Gammage* 37 Ch. D. 517.)	To any grandchild, or any number of them not exceeding three.
Grandchildren (daughters of a son, and sons of a daughter)	All to granddaughters equally	Equally *per stirpes*	To any grandchild, or any number of them not exceeding three.
Grandchildren (sons and daughters of a daughter, and daughters of another daughter)	Half to eldest son of one daughter, and half equally between daughters of other daughter	Equally *per stirpes*	To any grandchild, or any number of them not exceeding three.
Deceased son's widow, and child (*Bridge v. Abbot*, 3 *Bro. C.C.* 226)	All to child	All to child	Child.
Grandchild and great-grandchild, elder male branch	Great-grandchild	Equally	Grandchild.
Father and mother and brothers and sister	All to father	All to father	Father.
Mother and brothers and sisters	All to eldest brother	Equally	Mother.
Mother and sister	All to sister	Equally	Mother.
Mother only.	All (in default of any heirs on father's side)	All	Mother.
Brothers and sisters, and nephews and nieces (children of deceased sisters and younger brothers)	All to eldest brother	Equally, but nephews and nieces take *per stirpes*	To one or more of the brothers or sisters, not exceeding three.
Sisters, and nephews, and nieces (children of deceased brother)	All to nephew (eldest son of deceased brother)	Equally, but nephews and nieces take *per stirpes.*	To one or more of the sisters, not exceeding three.
Sisters, and nieces (children of deceased brother)	All to nieces equally	Equally, but nieces take *per stirpes*	To one or more of the sisters, not exceeding three.
Sisters, and nephews and nieces (children of deceased sister)	Equally between sisters and nephew, eldest son of deceased sister	Equally, but nephews and nieces take *per stirpes*	To one or more of the sisters not exceeding three.
Sisters, and nieces (children of deceased sister)	Equally, but nieces take *per stirpes*	Equally, but nieces take *per stirpes*	To one or more of the sisters, not exceeding three.

If a Person die leaving	LAND.—Real Property (except leaseholds) would descend	MONEY.—Personal Property (including leaseholds) would be divided	Persons entitled to administration.
Brother or sister of whole blood, and brother or sister of half-blood on father's side, and brother or sister of half-blood on mother's side	All to brother or sister of whole blood	Equally	Either or both.
Brother or sister of half-blood on father's side, and distant cousin on father's side	All to half-brother or sister	All to half-brother or sister	Brother or sister of half-blood.
Brother or sister of half-blood on mother's side, and distant cousin on father's side	All to distant cousin on father's side	All to half-brother or sister	Brother or sister of half-blood.
Brothers and sisters, and grandfather or grandmother	All to eldest brother	Equally between brothers and sisters (*Evelyn v. Evelyn*, 3 Atk. 762)	To one or more of brothers and sisters, not exceeding three.
Nephews and nieces by deceased brother, and nephew and nieces by deceased sister	All to eldest nephew (son of deceased brother)	Equally *per capita* (*i.e.*, shared equally without reference to the number of each family)	To either of the nephews or nieces, or any number of one or both, not exceeding three.
Nieces by deceased brother, and nephews and nieces by deceased sister	All to nieces (daughters of deceased brother)	Equally *per capita*	To either of the nephews or nieces, or any number of one or both, not exceeding three.
Nephews and nieces by one deceased sister and nieces by another deceased sister	Half to eldest nephew by one deceased sister, and half equally between nieces by other deceased sister	Equally *per capita*	To either of the nephews or nieces, or any number of one or both, not exceeding three.
Nephew (son of deceased sister) and great-niece, granddaughter of deceased brother	Great-niece	Nephew (*Pett v. Pett*, 1 Salk. 250)	Nephew.
Niece (brother or sister's daughter) and great-nephew (eldest brother's grandson)	All to great-nephew, eldest brother's grandson	All to niece, brother's or sister's daughter	Niece.
Father's father, or mother and mother's father or mother	All to father's father or (in default of heirs of father's father) to father's mother	Equally (*Moor v. Badham*, cited in *Blackborough v. Davis*, P. Wms. 53)	To either or both.
Grandfather, great-grandfather, uncle and aunt on father's side, and grandfather, uncle, and aunt, on mother's side	All to grandfather, on father's side	Equally between two grandfathers	To either or both grandfathers.

If a Person die leaving	LAND.—Real Property (except leaseholds) would descend	MONEY.—Personal Property (including leaseholds) would be divided	Persons entitled to administration.
Grandfather on mother's side, and uncle or aunt on father's side	All to uncle or aunt	All to grandfather	Grandfather.
Grandmother on either side, and uncle or aunt on father's side	All to uncle or aunt	All to grandmother (*Mentney v. Petty, Prec. Chan.*, 593)	Grandmother.
Grandmother on father's side, and uncle or aunt on mother's side	All to grandmother	All to grandmother (*Mentney v. Petty, Prec. Chan.*, 593)	Grandmother.
Great-grandfather, uncles and aunts on father's side	All to eldest uncle	Equally, *per capita*, (*Lloyd v. Tench,* 2 *Ves. Sen.*, 215)	To either or any number not exceeding three of either or both.
Uncles and aunts on mother's side, and nephews (sons of deceased sister) and nieces (daughters of a deceased brother)	Equally between nieces, daughters of brother	Equally *per capita*	To either or any number not exceeding three of either or both.
Uncles and aunts on father's side, and uncles and aunts on mother's side	All to eldest uncle on father's side	Equally among them	To either or any number not exceeding three of either or both.
Aunts on father's side, and uncles or aunts on mother's side	All equally to aunts on father's side	Equally among them	To either or any number not exceeding three of either or both.
Cousins	The eldest son of the deceased father's eldest brother (or according to heirship, as the case may be)	Equally *per capita*	To either or any number not exceeding three of either or both.
Uncle on mother's side, and cousin (son of another uncle on father's side)	All to cousin	All to uncle	Uncle.
No relations	All to the Crown (copyholds would go to the Lord of the Manor)	All to the Crown	To the Crown, or to a creditor, should he apply.

Note A.—The wife is only entitled to the third of the gross rental of the real estate for life as her dower, but in most cases this is barred, rather as a matter of form by lawyers, than for any other reason, and she then takes no interest in the real estate.

Note B.—This only applies to real estate in possession; the husband would take no benefit from his wife's reversionary interests in real estate.

Note C.—Children who have had advances from the *father* in the lifetime are to bring them into account.

Note D.—The above table to successions to real property does not extend to the decease of any person dying before 1st January, 1834, nor to Gavelkind lands in Kent and other places, nor to land held subject to Borough English custom, nor to Copyholds, nor to estates Tail.

Note E.—The husband is entitled in his marital right and not under the Statute of Distributions. He would, therefore, be excluded from taking any share of his wife's effects if given by any deed or will to "her next of kin" at her decease.—*Milne v. Gilbert, L. J., vol. 23, N. S. Chy.* 828.

Note F.—17 & 48 Vict., c. 71, s. 4, extends the law of escheat to any estate or interest in land whether legal or equitable.

INDEX.

BOND,
administration (will), 61.
by married woman, 61.
foreign sureties, 62.
sureties cannot be discharged, 62.
stamp on, 62.
by Guarantee Society, 62.
form of, 63.
attestation of, 65.
execution of, 65.
alterations in, 66.
administration, 83.
for resealing Colonial grant, 109, 110.

BRITISH POSSESSION,
property in, 31.
resealing grant from, 105.

BRITISH SUBJECT,
will of, 8.
affidavit as to status, 131.

BROTHER,
grant to, 68, 78, 80.

CALENDARS, 123.

CAVEAT, 116.
warning to, 117.
subducting, 117.
form of caveat, 133.

CERTIFICATE,
of delay, 7, 47.
form of, 132.

CESSATE GRANTS,
probates, 90.
administration (will), 91.
administrations, 92.

CHANNEL ISLANDS,
property in, 30.

CHILD,
administration by, 67, 76, 78.

"CLERK," 12, 64.

CODICIL,
execution of, 1, 2.
number of, to be stated in oath, 13.
affidavit as to execution, 125-127.
rules as to wills apply to, 145.

COLLATING DOCUMENTS, 122.

COLONIAL GRANTS, 105-110.

COLONIES,
    oaths in, 20.

COMMISSIONER FOR OATHS, 20.
    in administration cases must take oath and attest bond, 49, 65.

CORRECTIVE AFFIDAVIT, 38, 111.

COSTS,
    taxation of, 167.
    precedents of, 168-175.

COUSIN-GERMAN,
    grant to, 68, 81, 82.

CREDITOR,
    grant of administration (will) to, 57.
    of administration to, 82.

CUSTOMS AND INLAND REVENUE ACT, 1881, 21.

DATE OF DEATH OF DECEASED, 14.

DATE OF WILL, 7, 8.

DE BONIS NON GRANTS,
    administration (will), 94.
    administrations, 97.

DEBTS OF DECEASED,
    deducted in affidavit for Inland Revenue, 22, 30.

DECLARATION OF PERSONAL ESTATE,
    by guardian, 71.
    by next of kin of lunatic, 74.
    form of, 133.

DEEDS,
    incorporated in will, 5, 144.

DELAY,
    to be explained, 7, 47, 69, 111.
    certificate of, 132.

DEPONENT,
    blind or illiterate, 18, 19.

DESCRIPTION,
    of testator, 13.
    of sureties to bond, 63.
    of next of kin, 76.

DISTRICT REGISTRIES, 176.

NEXT-OF-KIN,
    administration (will) to, 47.
    description of, 67, 68.
    table of, 178.

NOTATION,
    of domicile, 101.
        form of affidavit, 134.
    after grant passed, 101.
        form of affidavit, 134.

OATH,
    for executors, 11.
    for administrators (with will), 48.
        to guardian of minor, 58, 59.
        to attorney, 60.
    for administration to guardian of minors, 72.
        to guardian of infant, 73.
        to attorney, 74.
        to next-of-kin of lunatic, 74.
    for administrators, 75.
    for administration to official receiver, 82.
    for administration to creditor, 82.
    for double probate, 87.
    for cessate probate, 90.
    for cessate administration (will), 91.
    for cessate administrators, 93.
    for administration (will) *de bonis non*, 95, 96.
    for administration *de bonis non*, 98, 99.
    for re-sealing Colonial grant, 108.
    to lead substituted grant, 115.
    for noting domicile when grant passes, 134.
    for noting domicile after probate, 134.

OATHS,
    who may administer, 20.
        in Scotland, 20.
        in Ireland, 20.
        in Colonies, 20.
        in foreign parts, 20.

OFFICE COPY WILLS, 120.

OFFICIAL RECEIVER,
    grant to, 82.

ORDERS AND RULES, 140-167.

PERSONAL ESTATE,
    gross value to be inserted in oath, 17.
    grant given in respect of all of which deceased died possessed, 18.
    in Scotland, 18.
    in Ireland, 18, 104.
    abroad, 30.

PLACE OF DEATH, 14.

O

WILL.—*(continued)*.
    copy of, sworn to, 10, 13.
    transmission of original, 123.
    affidavit as to alterations in, 125.
    affidavits by witnesses to, 125, 127.
    affidavit as to validity, 129.

WILLS ACT, 1837, 1, 3.

WILLS ACT, 1852, 3.

WILLS ACT, 1861, 8.

WITNESS,
    to will, 1.
    to codicil, 1, 2.
    affidavit by, as to execution, 2, 3, 126.
        as to reading over, 2, 127.
        as to alterations, 4, 125.
        as to date of will, 7, 8.
        as to plight, 131.
    if both dead, affidavit as to execution, 4.
    forms of affidavit by, 125-127.

"YOUNGER," 13.

LIST

OF

LEGAL AND GENERAL BOOKS

PRINTED AND PUBLISHED

BY

WATERLOW & SONS LIMITED,

LAW, PARLIAMENTARY AND GENERAL STATIONERS, PRINTERS, &c.,

85 & 86, LONDON WALL;

FINSBURY STATIONERY WORKS, E.C.;

AND

49, PARLIAMENT STREET, S.W.,

ETC., ETC.,

LONDON.

———

BRANCH OFFICE: TEMPLE ROW, BIRMINGHAM.

500
10-6-97.

LIST OF PUBLICATIONS.

AGRICULTURAL HOLDINGS (ENGLAND) ACT, 1883, with Notes and Forms, and a Summary of the Procedure. By J. W. JEUDWINE, of Lincoln's Inn, Barrister-at-Law. Second Edition, revised and enlarged. In cloth, 3s. 6d.

BANKERS', INSURANCE MANAGERS' AND AGENTS' MAGAZINE.—A First Class Monthly Financial Publication, and the recognized organ of communication for the Banking interest. 1s. 6d. per number, or 21s. per annum, including two double numbers.

BANKING ALMANAC, DIRECTORY, AND DIARY.—A Year Book of Statistics and complete Banking Directory. The Edition for 1897 is the 53rd year of publication of this invaluable book, which has long been patronized by the Bank of England and the Private and Joint Stock Banks throughout the Kingdom. In cloth, 12s. 6d. net.

BANKRUPTCY ACTS, 1883 TO 1890, with the General Rules, Forms, Scales of Costs, Fees and Percentages, Board of Trade and Court Orders, Debtors Act, 1869, Deeds of Arrangement Act, 1887, Rules as to Administration Orders, &c., and a Commentary thereon. By His Honour Judge CHALMERS and E. HOUGH, Inspector in Bankruptcy, Board of Trade. Fourth Edition, revised to October, 1896. By M. MUIR MACKENZIE, Barrister-at-Law, and E. HOUGH. In cloth, 25s.

BILLS OF EXCHANGE ACT, 1882.—An Act to Codify the Law relating to Bills of Exchange, Cheques, and Promissory Notes. With Comments and Explanatory Notes. By His Honour Judge CHALMERS. Eighth Edition. In cloth, 3s. 6d.

CODE OF CONTRACT LAW, relating to Sales of Goods of the value of £10 and upwards. A Handbook for the use of professional and business men. By HENRY J. PARRINGTON, of Middlesbrough, Solicitor. In cloth, 3s. 6d.

CODE OF THE LAW OF RATING AND PROCEDURE ON APPEAL, with an Appendix containing all the Statutes (including the Agricultural Rates Act, 1896), fully annotated, and Specimens of Valuations made for the Purposes of Rating. By SYLVAIN MAYER. B.A., PH.D., of the Middle Temple and Northern Circuit, Barrister-at-Law ; Author of " The French Code of Commerce," etc. In 1 vol., Royal 8vo., about 600 pages, 25s.

COMPUTATOR.—A Treatise and Ready-Help for the young Banker's or Accountant's Clerk. With tables, &c. By A. WALKER. In cloth, 1s.

COUNTRY BANKERS' HANDBOOK to the Rules and Practices of (I.) the Bank of England, (II.) London Bankers' Clearing House, (III.) the Stock Exchange. With useful Miscellaneous Notes. By J. GEORGE KIDDY. Second Edition. In cloth, 2s. 6d.

CRIMINAL LAW AMENDMENT ACT, 1885, with Preface and Commentary. By R. W. BURNIE, of the Middle Temple, Barrister-at-Law. In boards, 2s. 6d.

COUNTY COUNCIL COMPENDIUM; OR DIGEST OF THE MUNICIPAL CORPORATIONS ACT, 1882; THE COUNTY ELECTORS AND LOCAL GOVERNMENT ACTS, 1888.—Being a Treatise on the above Statutes and others re-enacted therein. With Copious Notes and Appendices, &c. Second Edition. By HENRY STEPHEN and HORACE E. MILLER, LL.B., Barristers-at-Law. In cloth, 21s.

LIST OF PUBLICATIONS—CONTINUED.

COUNTY COUNCILLORS' VADE-MECUM.—A Handbook for County Councillors and Aldermen. By HENRY STEPHEN and HORACE MILLER, LL.B., Authors of "The County Council Compendium." Crown 8vo. In cloth, 2s. 6d.

COUNTY COUNCILS, MUNICIPAL CORPORATIONS AND LOCAL AUTHORITIES COMPANION AND DIARY.—The most complete work of reference in connection with County and Borough Administration extant. Compiled and edited by Sir J. R. SOMERS VINE, C.M.G., F.R.G.S., F.S.S. Two Editions, with Diary 3 days to a page. No. 1, bound in cloth, lettered, 10s. 6d. No. 2, bound in crimson morocco, gilt edges, &c., and Subscriber's name lettered on cover, 15s.

COUNTY COURTS ACT, 1888.—Queen's Printers' Copy, with an introduction indicating the leading alterations made by the Act, a Comprehensive Index, &c., &c., and the County Courts Admiralty Jurisdiction Acts, 1868 and 1869, with a separate Index, by R. T. HUNTER, Chief Clerk, County Court, Stockton-on-Tees. Second Edition. In boards, cloth backs, 5s. The same may be had with the Act Interleaved for Notes. In boards, 6s.

COUNTY COURT RULES, 1889, with an Index to the Pages, Orders, Rules, Forms, and Fees, an Alphabetical List of Forms (referring to page, order, and rule), and Tables showing the Fees and Costs on any given sum. By R. T. HUNTER, Chief Clerk, County Court, Stockton-on-Tees. In boards, 7s., or in roan, 10s. 6d. The same Index in separate form, in boards, 3s. 6d.

COSTS IN THE COUNTY COURTS under the County Courts Act, 1888, and Rules of 1889 and 1892, with the Sections and Rules relating thereto and Precedents. By R. T. HUNTER, Chief Clerk, County Court, Stockton-on-Tees. Price 6s.

DEBTORS AND CREDITORS.—A Guide to the Proceedings for Recovery of Debt by Action in the County Courts or in the High Court, and the Administration of Insolvent Estates, showing the position of Debtors and Creditors under the various proceedings. By ERNEST SAVILLE, of the Bankruptcy Department, Board of Trade. In cloth, 3s. 6d.

DEEDS OF ARRANGEMENT ACT, 1887, AND THE BANKRUPTCY (DISCHARGE AND CLOSURE) ACT, 1887, with Rules, Forms, and Scales of Fees prescribed thereunder; also with Notes and Index. By His Honour Judge CHALMERS and E. HOUGH, Inspector in Bankruptcy, Board of Trade. In cloth, 3s. 6d.

DUE DATE TABLES FOR ACCEPTING BILLS OF EXCHANGE.—Compiled by HENRY BELL and JOHN MONTGOMERY, JR. These Tables are most useful to Bankers, Merchants, Manufacturers and others, are perpetually serviceable, and suffer no alteration from year to year. In cloth, 7s. 6d.

DUTIES OF EXECUTORS.—By F. W. DENDY, Solicitor and Notary. Sixth Edition. Revised in accordance with the Finance Act, 1894. Post free, 1s. 8d.

ELECTORAL BOUNDARIES OF THE UNITED KINGDOM, being Schedules 5, 6, and 7 of the Parliamentary Elections (Redistribution) Act, 1885. With Index. In boards, 2s. 6d.

LIST OF PUBLICATIONS—CONTINUED.

ENGLISH MUNICIPAL CODE, or the MUNICIPAL CORPORATIONS (Consolidation) ACT, 1882, with Statutes and Cases from 1882 to 1888, Notes, Comments, References, Statistical Appendix, and Voluminous Index, by Sir J. R. SOMERS VINE, C.M.G., F.R.G.S., F.S.S. Third Edition. In cloth, 7s. 6d.

ENGLISH MUNICIPAL INSTITUTIONS: THEIR GROWTH AND DEVELOPMENT STATISTICALLY ILLUSTRATED.—"A most useful and valuable work."—*Vide* Public Press. By Sir J. R. SOMERS VINE, C.M.G., F.R.G.S., F.S.S. Royal 8vo, cloth, 10s. 6d.

FORM OF BILLS OF SALE UNDER THE BILLS OF SALE ACT (1878) AMENDMENT ACT, 1882.—By STANLEY BUCKMASTER, M.A., of the Inner Temple, Barrister-at-Law. In cloth, 2s. 6d.

FRANCHISE ACTS, 1884-5, being the Representation of the People Act, 1884; Registration Act, 1885; Parliamentary Elections (Redistribution) Act, 1885, and Medical Relief Disqualification Removal Act, 1885, with Introduction and Notes. By MILES WALKER MATTINSON, Barrister-at-Law. In boards, 2s. 6d.

GENERAL RAILWAY ACTS, 1830–1884.—A Collection of the Public General Acts for the Regulation of Railways, including the Companies, Lands, and Railways Clauses Consolidation Acts. Fourteenth Edition, as amended to close of the Session 1884. By JAS. BIGG, Esq. In cloth, 21s.

GUIDE TO THE LAW AND PRACTICE OF PETTY SESSIONS, with the Summary Jurisdiction Act, 1879. By EDWARD T. AYERS, Solicitor and late Assistant Clerk to Justices, Great Yarmouth. In cloth, 5s.

GUIDE TO THE LAW OF DISTRESS FOR RENT.—A Handbook for Landlords, Land Agents, Certified Bailiffs, and others. By R. T. HUNTER, Chief Clerk, County Court, Stockton-on-Tees. Seventh Edition. In cloth, 3s. 6d. net.

GUIDE TO THE PREPARATION OF BILLS OF COSTS (PRIDMORE'S), containing Practical Directions for Taxing Costs, and complete Precedents of Bills of Costs in all the Divisions, in conformity with the present Practice. Ninth Edition. By CHAS. W. SCOTT, one of the principal Clerks in the Chancery Taxing Office, Royal Courts of Justice. In cloth, 25s.

HANDBOOK OF THE LAW RELATING TO THE MANAGEMENT OF PARLIAMENTARY, COUNTY COUNCIL AND MUNICIPAL ELECTIONS.—A statement of the Law relating to the machinery of Elections. Second Edition. By H. STEPHEN, Barrister-at-Law. In cloth, 1s.

HANDBOOK TO THE ESTATE DUTY, comprising the Finance Acts, 1894 and 1896 with a comment thereon, an Appendix of Forms, Duties, &c., and an Index. By ALFRED W. SOWARD, of the Legacy and Succession Duty Office, Somerset House. Second Edition. In cloth, 5s. net.

LIST OF PUBLICATIONS—CONTINUED.

HANDBOOK TO THE SMALL HOLDINGS ACT, 1892, AND THE STATUTORY PROVISIONS INCORPORATED THEREIN.—By HORACE E. MILLER, LL.B., Barrister-at-Law. In cloth, 2s. 6d.

HANDBOOK TO THE STAMP DUTIES, containing the Text of the Stamp Act, 1891, and a complete Alphabetical Table of all documents liable to Stamp Duty. By H. S. BOND, Esq., of the Solicitor's Department, Inland Revenue, Somerset House. Ninth Edition. Post free, 2s.

HIRE-PURCHASE SYSTEM.—An Epitome of the Law relating to all matters connected with Hire-Purchase Agreements, and having special reference to the decision of the House of Lords in "Helby v. Matthews." By WILLIAM H. RUSSELL, Solicitor, Cheltenham. In cloth, 2s. 6d. net.

INDIAN EXCHANGE TABLES.—By J. I. BERRY. In cloth, 21s., or with Supplement 25s.

    SUPPLEMENT TO DITTO, 5s.

    SECOND SUPPLEMENT TO DITTO, 5s.

INTEREST TABLES at the rate of two and three-quarters per cent. per annum on sums varying from £1 to £10,000 for all periods from 1 to 364 days, and from 1 to 12 months. Compiled by F. ALBAN BARRAUD, Solicitor. In cloth, 2s. 6d.

JOINT-STOCK COMPANIES' PRACTICAL GUIDE. — By HENRY HURRELL and CLARENDON G. HYDE, Barristers-at-Law. Invaluable to the Legal Profession, and to Secretaries, Directors, Promoters, and all other persons engaged in the formation or management of Joint-Stock Companies. Fifth Edition. In cloth, 5s.

LAW AND PROCEDURE OF SUMMARY JUDGMENT ON SPECIALLY INDORSED WRIT, under Order XIV. By C. CAVANAGH, of the Middle Temple, Barrister-at-Law. In cloth, 5s. net.

LAW AND PRACTICE OF REGISTRATION OF DEEDS IN THE COUNTY OF MIDDLESEX under the Middlesex Deeds Acts, containing the full texts of the Acts, Rules and Fee Order with Notes, Instructions, Precedents of Memorials, &c. By C. FORTESCUE-BRICKDALE, of Lincoln's Inn, Barrister-at-Law. In cloth, 3s. 6d.

LAW OF BUILDING, ENGINEERING, AND SHIP BUILDING CONTRACTS.—By ALFRED A. HUDSON, of the Inner Temple, Barrister-at-Law. Second Edition, in 2 vols., 50s.

LAW OF DIRECTORS AND OFFICERS OF JOINT STOCK COMPANIES, their Powers Duties, and Liabilities. By HENRY HURRELL, of the Middle Temple, and CLARENDON G. HYDE, of the Middle Temple, Barristers-at-Law. Third Edition. In cloth, 6s.

LAW OF MERCANTILE AGENTS; OR, THE FACTORS ACT, 1889.—By M. MOLONEY Barrister-at-Law. In cloth boards, post free, 1s. 7d.

LIST OF PUBLICATIONS—CONTINUED.

LAW OF MERCHANT SHIPPING AND FREIGHT, with Tables of Cases, Forms, and Complete Index. By J. T. FOARD, of the Inner Temple, Barrister-at-Law. Royal 8vo. In half-calf, 21s.

LAW OF RATES AND CHARGES ON RAILWAYS AND CANALS.—Synopsis of the Railway and Canal Traffic Act, 1888. By PERCY GYE and THOS. WAGHORN, of the Inner Temple, Barristers-at-Law. In boards, 2s. In cloth, 3s.

LAW RELATING TO BETTING, TIME BARGAINS AND GAMING, including the Law relating to Stakeholders, Stewards, the Winners of Races; Stock Exchange Transactions; Lotteries, Gaming Houses, Betting Houses, &c. By GEORGE HERBERT STUTFIELD and HENRY S. CAUTLEY, Barristers-at-Law. Third Edition, revised and enlarged. In boards, 2s. 6d.

LAW RELATING TO CORRUPT PRACTICES AT PARLIAMENTARY, MUNICIPAL AND OTHER ELECTIONS, AND THE PRACTICE ON ELECTION PETITIONS, with an Appendix of Statutes, Rules and Forms. By MILES WALKER MATTINSON and STUART CUNNINGHAM MACASKIE, of Gray's Inn, Barristers-at-Law. Third Edition. In cloth, 10s.

LEGAL ADVICE to Engineers, Architects, Surveyors, Contractors, and Employers. By A. A. HUDSON, Barrister-at-Law. Post free, 1s. 7d.

LOCAL GOVERNMENT ACT, 1894.—Queen's Printers' Copy, with an exhaustive Index. By HORACE E. MILLER, LL.B., Barrister-at-Law. Post free, 2s. 3d.

MANUAL OF HYDROLOGY.—By N. BEARDMORE, C.E. In cloth, 24s.

MANUAL OF THEATRICAL LAW, containing Instructions for Licensing Theatres and Music Halls, and Chapters on the Law of Contracts between Actors and Managers, &c., &c. By CLARENCE HAMLYN, of the Middle Temple, Barrister-at-Law. In cloth, 5s.

MERCATOR'S BUSINESS AND SOCIAL TELEGRAPHIC POCKET CODE.—Compiled by Practical Telegraphist. In cloth, 5s. net.

MERCHANDISE MARKS ACTS, 1887 and 1891, with Commentaries, Decided Cases, and references to Expert Evidence before Select Committees. By FRANK SAFFORD, of the Middle Temple, Barrister-at-Law. In cloth, 7s. 6d.

ORGANIZATION OF A SOLICITOR'S OFFICE, being a reprint (with revisions) of a Series of Articles contributed to the "Solicitors' Journal." By EDWARD F. TURNER, Solicitor. Third Edition. In cloth, 7s. 6d.

PARISH AND DISTRICT COUNCILS.—A Treatise on the Local Government Act, 1894, with the incorporated Provisions of other Acts, and the Orders and Circulars issued by the Local Government Board. By HORACE E. MILLER, LL.B., Barrister-at-Law. In cloth, 7s. 6d.

POSITION IN LAW OF WOMEN.—Showing how it differs from that of Men, and the effect of the Married Women's Property Act, 1882. By THOMAS BARRETT-LENNARD, of the Middle Temple, Barrister-at Law. In cloth, 6s.

LIST OF PUBLICATIONS—CONTINUED.

PRACTICAL HINTS ON THE PREPARATION AND REGISTRATION of Joint-Stock Companies' Forms, with Precedents, Tables of Fees and Stamp Duties and an Index. Third Edition. Post free, 1s. 8d.

PRACTICAL SUGGESTIONS ON THE PREPARATION AND REGISTRATION OF DEEDS and other Documents at the various Public Offices, with Tables of Fees and an Index. Second Edition. Post free, 1s. 8d.

PRACTICE OF THE LAND REGISTRY UNDER THE TRANSFER OF LAND ACT, 1862, with such portions of the Rules as are now in force, General Instructions, Notes, Forms, and Precedents. By CHARLES FORTESCUE-BRICKDALE, B.A., of Lincoln's Inn, Barrister, Assisting Barrister to the Land Registry. In cloth, 3s. 6d.

PRACTITIONER'S PROBATE MANUAL.—Containing Instructions as to Procedure in obtaining Grants of Probate and Administration, with numerous Precedents of Forms, and full particulars as to Duties, Fees, &c., with a copious Index. Fifth Edition. In cloth, 5s. net.

RAILWAYS IN SCOTLAND, 1845-1873.—The General Acts for the Regulation of Railways in Scotland, including the Companies, Lands and Railways Clauses (Scotland) Acts, complete to the close of 1873, and a copious Index. A Supplement to the General Railway Acts. 12mo. In cloth (1873), 5s.

RELATIONSHIP OF LANDLORD AND TENANT.—By EDGAR FOA, Barrister-at-Law. Second Edition. In cloth, 25s.

RIGHTS AND DUTIES OF TRUSTEES IN BANKRUPTCY AND UNDER DEEDS OF ARRANGEMENT, containing Information as to Appointment and Security, Realizing and Distributing the Property of Estates. Administration of Estates and Rendering of Accounts to the Board of Trade by Trustees under Deeds of Arrangement; and a Time Table showing the time at which the principal Duties of Trustees are to be performed. By H. F. WREFORD. In cloth, 3s. 6d.

SHORT AND CONCISE PRECEDENTS OF THE CLAUSES MOST GENERALLY IN USE IN FARMING AGREEMENTS, with complete Forms of Agreements, Dissertations, and Full Notes, and a Table of Contents. By J. W. JEUDWINE, of Lincoln's Inn, Barrister-at-Law. In boards, 2s.

SOLICITORS' DIARY, ALMANAC, LEGAL DIGEST, AND DIRECTORY.—The Edition for 1897 is the 53rd year of publication of this important Annual, which is now universally recognized as the most useful Legal Diary published. Prices— 3s. 6d., 5s., 6s., and 8s. 6d., according to diary space and binding.

SOLICITORS' POCKET BOOK.—In leather tuck, 2s. 6d.; roan wallet, 4s. 6d.; and Russia wallet, 7s. 6d.

LIST OF PUBLICATIONS—CONTINUED.

STANDING ORDERS.—The Standing Orders of the Lords and Commons relative to Private Bills, with Appendix. Published at the close of each Session. In cloth, 5s.

SUMMARY JURISDICTION ACT, 1884, with Notes. A Supplement to Ayers' " Guide to the Law and Practice of Petty Sessions." By EDWARD T. AYERS, Solicitor. In boards, 2s.

SUMMARY JURISDICTION ACTS.—Tabular View of the Summary Jurisdiction of Justices as to Indictable Offences. By E. T. AYERS, Solicitor, Great Yarmouth. Printed on indestructible paper, 2s. net.

STOCK EXCHANGE ACCOUNTS, with an Appendix of Forms. By STEPHEN H. M. KILLIK. In cloth, 3s. 6d. net.

TABLE OF CORRUPT AND ILLEGAL PRACTICES WHICH VITIATE THE ELECTION. By M. W. MATTINSON and S. C. MACASKIE, Barristers-at-Law. On linen-lined card. Prices: 1 copy, 2d.; 50 copies, 6s.; 100 copies, 10s. May also be had printed on stout cardboard, 11 × 17. suitable for affixing to the walls of Committee Rooms. Price 6d. each.

TABLE OF FEES, CHARGES AND EXPENSES, AND COURT FEES, UNDER THE LAW OF DISTRESS AMENDMENT ACT, 1888.—Stamp Duty on Appraisement, Fees Chargeable by High Bailiffs, &c. By R. T. HUNTER, Chief Clerk, County Court, Stockton-on-Tees. Mounted on linen and folded in cloth case, 1s. 6d.

TABLES FOR THE IMMEDIATE CONVERSION OF PRODUCTS INTO INTEREST AT TWENTY-NINE RATES, viz.:—from one to eight per cent. inclusive, &c., &c. By A. CROSBIE and W. C. LAW. Second Edition. Improved and enlarged. In roan, 12s. 6d.

TRUSTEE ACT, 1893, including a Guide for Trustees to Investments. By ARTHUR LEE ELLIS, of Lincoln's Inn, Barrister-at-Law. Fifth Edition. In cloth, 6s.

WATERLOW'S BIJOU AND CONDENSED DIARIES.—Published in October. These elegant and useful Pocket Diaries are issued in two sizes, series Y, 3¼ × 2¼ series Z, 4¼ × 2¼, artistically printed in two colours on metallic paper, and can be had in paper covers at 1s. 6d. and 1s. 9d. each, and covered in silk at 2s. and 2s. 6d. each, or in roan, morocco, Russian or crocodile wallets, from 5s. each.

WATERLOW'S SCRIBBLING DIARY. Foolscap folio, 6 days on a page, interleaved, strong paper cover, 1s.; 3 days, 1s. 6d. ; 2 days. ½ bound cloth, 3s. ; 1 day, 5s.

PRACTICAL SUGGESTIONS

PREPARATION

AND

REGISTRATION OF DEEDS

AND OTHER DOCUMENTS,

AT THE VARIOUS PUBLIC OFFICES,

WITH

TABLES OF FEES

AND AN

INDEX.

Second Edition.

POST FREE, ONE SHILLING AND EIGHT PENCE.

PRACTICAL HINTS

ON THE

PREPARATION AND REGISTRATION

OF

Joint Stock Companies' Forms,

WITH

Precedents, Table of Fees and Stamp Duties, and an Index.

Third Edition.

POST FREE, ONE SHILLING AND EIGHT PENCE.

85 & 86, LONDON WALL, LONDON.

9

Handbook

TO THE

ESTATE DUTY

COMPRISING

The Finance Acts, 1894 and 1896,

WITH

A LENGTHY COMMENT THEREON,

An Appendix of Forms, Duties, and Fees on taking out Grants,

AND AN

INDEX.

BY

ALFRED W. SOWARD,

Of the Legacy and Succession Duty Office, Somerset House.

The Finance Act, 1894, is admittedly one of the most difficult and complicated fiscal measures, both legally and financially, which has ever been under the consideration of Parliament. It effects radical and far-reaching changes in the Law and Practice of the Death Duties, and renders a supplement to existing text-books on the Duties indispensably necessary.

The handbook contains the text of the Estate Duty, parts of the Acts in full, with an explanatory comment showing the scope and operation of the new Laws; it also includes PRACTICAL INSTRUCTIONS for the delivery of Affidavits and Accounts, and the payment and rectification of Duty. There is an Appendix of Forms, Duties and Fees, and a full Index.

Second Edition in Cloth, 5s. net.

---

85 & 86, LONDON WALL, LONDON.

THE PRACTITIONER'S

PROBATE MANUAL,

CONTAINING

INSTRUCTIONS AS TO PROCEDURE IN OBTAINING GRANTS OF PROBATE AND ADMINISTRATION,

WITH

NUMEROUS PRECEDENTS OF FORMS,

AND

Full Particulars as to Duties, Fees, &c.,

WITH A

SUPPLEMENT,

SHEWING ALTERATIONS EFFECTED BY THE FINANCE ACT, 1896,

AND A

COPIOUS INDEX.

FIFTH EDITION.

In cloth, FIVE Shillings net.

85 & 86, LONDON WALL, LONDON.

11

PRICE LIST OF PARCHMENT.

PLAIN.

When ordering, the full size of Skin should always be given.		ORDINARY QUALITY.		BEST SELECTED.	
		Each.	Per doz.	Each.	Per doz.
Depth.	Width.	s. d.	s. d.	s. d.	s. d.
8½ ×	13	0 4	3 6	0 5	4 6
10½ ×	17	0 9	8 0	0 10	9 0
12 ×	16	0 9	8 0	0 10	9 0
10½ ×	21	0 10	9 6	1 0	11 0
13 ×	17	0 10	9 6	1 0	11 0
15 ×	20	1 0	11 6	1 2	12 6
16 ×	21	1 2	13 0	1 4	14 6
17 ×	22	1 4	15 0	1 6	16 6
18 ×	24	1 6	17 6	1 8	19 0
19 ×	25	1 10	20 0	2 0	22 0
22 ×	27	2 0	22 0	2 3	25 0
23 ×	28	2 3	25 0	2 6	28 0
26 ×	29	2 6	28 6	2 9	31 0
27 ×	30	2 9	31 6	3 0	34 0
28 ×	32	3 3	35 0	3 6	37 0

Larger sizes can be supplied.

INDENTURES AND FOLLOWERS.

RED LINED AND RULED OR RED LINED ONLY.

When ordering, the full size of Skin should always be given.			ORDINARY QUALITY.		BEST SELECTED.	
			Each.	Per doz.	Each.	Per doz.
			s. d.	s. d.	s. d.	s. d.
INDENTURES	Open	15 × 20	1 6	15 0	1 9	18 0
		19 × 25	2 6	26 0	2 9	28 0
		22 × 27	2 9	28 0	3 0	30 0
		26 × 29	3 0	30 0	3 6	36 0
		27 × 30	3 6	35 0	4 0	40 0
FOLLOWERS		23 × 28	2 6	26 0	3 0	30 0
		24 × 29	3 0	30 0	3 6	36 0
INDENTURES and FOLLOWERS	Bookway. Sizes before folding.	10½ × 17	1 0	10 6	1 2	12 0
		11½ × 18	1 2	12 0	1 4	13 6
		13 × 17	1 3	14 0	1 6	16 0
		16 × 21	1 9	18 0	2 0	21 0
		18 × 24	2 3	22 0	2 6	25 0
		19 × 25	2 6	26 0	2 9	28 0
		22 × 27	2 9	28 0	3 0	30 0

PRICE LIST OF PARCHMENT—*continued.*

PROBATES,
WITH OR WITHOUT HEADING, BLACK LINED AND RULED.

When ordering, the full size of Skin should always be given.	ORDINARY QUALITY.		BEST SELECTED.	
	Each.	Per doz.	Each.	Per doz.
	s. d.	s. d.	s. d.	s. d.
12 × 16 .	1 0	10 6	1 2	12 0
15 × 20 .	1 6	15 0	1 9	18 0
18 × 24 .	2 0	22 0	2 3	25 0
22 × 27 .	2 9	28 0	3 0	30 0
26 × 29 .	3 0	30 0	3 6	36 0
28 × 32 .	3 9	40 0	4 0	45 0

BOOKWAY PROBATES,
HEADED, RULED AND ENDORSED.

	ORDINARY QUALITY.		BEST SELECTED.	
	Each.	Per doz.	Each.	Per doz.
	s. d.	s. d.	s. d.	s. d.
Fronts (headed and ruled) 10 × 12	0 10	9 0	1 0	10 6
Insides (ruled only) 10 × 12	0 10	9 0	1 0	10 6
Backs (ruled and endorsed) 12 × 12	0 10	9 0	1 0	10 6
Do. (ruled only) 12 × 12	0 10	9 0	1 0	10 6
Fronts (headed and ruled) 10½ × 13½	1 0	10 6	1 2	12 0
Insides (ruled only) 10½ × 13½	1 0	10 6	1 2	12 0
Backs (ruled and endorsed) 10½ × 15	1 0	10 6	1 2	12 0
Do. (ruled only) . 10½ × 15	1 0	10 6	1 2	12 0

For Paper Indentures, see next page.

PAPER INDENTURES, AGREEMENTS, &c.,

PRINTED, RULED AND RED-LINED, WHEN NOT OTHERWISE DESCRIBED.

	Large Post 4to. Per Quire.		Medium 4to. Per Quire.		F'cap. Per Quire.		Demy. Per Quire.		Royal. Per Quire.	
	s.	d.	s.	d.	s.	d.	s.	d.	s.	d.
This Indenture . .	2	6	3	0	3	6	4	6	6	6
Ditto (ruled grey feint only)	—		—		—		4	0	6	0
Memorandum of Agreement . .	2	6	3	0	3	6	4	6	6	6
Ditto (ruled grey feint only)	—		—		3	0	4	0	—	
An Agreement . .	2	6	3	0	3	6	4	6	—	
Ditto (ruled grey feint only)	—		—		—		4	0	—	
Inventory and Valuation .	—		—		3	6	4	6	—	
Ditto (ruled grey feint only)	—		—		3	0	—		—	
Inventory (ditto)	—		—		3	0	—		—	
Valuation (ditto)	—		—		3	0	—		—	
Know all Men . .	2	6	—		3	6	4	6	—	
This is the Last Will and Testament (*not red lined*)	2	6	3	0	3	6	4	6	—	
Followers . . .	2	6	3	0	3	6	4	6	6	6

	s.	d.
This is the Last Will and Testament, on Lined Brief . per quire	2	6
This Indenture, on ditto ,,	2	6
Followers . . . . . ,,	1	4
Specification, on F'cap ½ sheets, ruled grey feint ,,	1	6
Followers on F'cap ½ sheets, ruled grey feint . ,,	1	6

LAW WRITING AND ENGROSSING.

WATERLOW & SONS LIMITED desire to call the attention of Solicitors to the facilities which they are enabled to offer for the execution of all classes of Legal Work.

A competent staff of law writers and clerks is constantly engaged at 85 and 86, London Wall, and at 49, Parliament Street, Westminster, and W. & S. Ld. are therefore enabled to execute any work entrusted to them with the utmost care and despatch.

DEEDS, etc., carefully and correctly engrossed.

STAMP DUTIES assessed and paid.

Charges for copying at per folio of 72 words—

	s.	d.
Engrossments in Round-hand	0	2
Attested Copies and Fair Copies of every description . . .	0	1½
Wills, Abstracts, Parliamentary Briefs and Minutes of Evidence	0	2
Abstracting Titles and Fair Copy	0	6

Drafts, etc., received from the country can be engrossed or copied and sent by return post when required.

A Large Stock of STAMPED PARCHMENT AND PAPER of every description being kept ready for immediate use, any order can be executed without the slightest delay.

LAW LITHOGRAPHY.

The facilities afforded by WATERLOW & SONS LIMITED in this department having led to so great an increase of their business, they are enabled to retain a staff of hands capable of completing, in a few hours, any amount of work however large.

Briefs, Abstracts, Minutes of Evidence, Reports and Legal Documents, Builders' Quantities, Contracts, Specifications, etc., lithographed in good plain round-hand, with the greatest accuracy.

A Brief of 100 sheets can, if necessary, be lithographed in three or four hours. The evidence taken daily on Private Bills or Arbitration Cases may be neatly and correctly lithographed or printed *during the night*, and delivered to Counsel *before 9 o'clock the following morning.*

The following prices are intended as a guide to the charges for the ordinary description of Law Lithography; where a great number of copies of any document are required, special estimates will be given.

Abstracts copied Briefwise, 5 to 8 folios, per sheet on Superfine Paper:—

8 Copies	.	.	.	6d. per sheet.
12 ,,	.	.	.	4½d. ,,
20 ,,	.	.	.	3½d. ,,
30 ,,	.	.	.	3d. ,,
50 ,,	.	.	.	2d. ,,
100 ,,	.	.	.	1½d. ,,

Per 100, after the first 100, 10s. 6d.

Drafts, 4 to 5 folios per page, on Superfine Laid Copy:—

10 Copies	.	.	.	4d. per page.
20 ,,	.	.	.	2½d. ,,
50 ,,	.	.	.	1½d. ,,
100 ,,	.	.	.	7s. 6d.

Per 100, after the first 100, 5s. 6d.

Deeds, Law Letters, and Forms Lithographed.

Where preferred, the charge will be made by the folio, in proportion to the above scale.

Minutes of Evidence and Parliamentary Documents are charged at 2d. per folio.

LAW AGENCY

AND

INLAND REVENUE STAMPING.

WATERLOW & SONS LIMITED devote special attention to this department, and are in daily attendance at Somerset House and the various Public Offices.

PAPERS LODGED FOR PROBATE AND ADMINISTRATION.

ESTATE DUTY, LEGACY, SUCCESSION AND RESIDUARY ACCOUNTS PASSED, AND DUTIES PAID.

PROBATES AND LETTERS OF ADMINISTRATION LODGED FOR REGISTRATION AT COMPANIES' OFFICES.

BILLS OF SALE AND DEEDS OF ARRANGEMENT STAMPED AND FILED.

JOINT-STOCK COMPANIES REGISTERED, AND ANNUAL SUMMARIES, SPECIAL RESOLUTIONS, etc., FILED.

DEEDS LODGED FOR ADJUDICATION OF STAMP DUTY.

ADVERTISEMENTS INSERTED IN THE "LONDON GAZETTE" AND OTHER LONDON PAPERS.

SEARCHES MADE AT ANY OF THE PUBLIC OFFICES WITH THE GREATEST CARE AND EXPEDITION.

DEEDS AND ALL EXECUTED INSTRUMENTS STAMPED AND FORWARDED BY RETURN OF POST, a small charge being made for attendance and postage. The greatest care is exercised in the assessment of Stamp Duty payable on any document entrusted to the Company for stamping, but they incur no responsibility in the event of an improper assessment being made.

WATERLOW & SONS LIMITED also attend to the

REGISTRATION OF COPYRIGHT BOOKS AND DRAWINGS,

AND TO THE

REGISTRATION OF TRADE-MARKS AND OF DESIGNS.

APPLICATIONS FOR PATENTS CONDUCTED UNDER THE PERSONAL SUPERVISION OF A FELLOW OF THE INSTITUTE OF PATENT AGENTS.

85 & 86, LONDON WALL, LONDON.

16

SUPPLEMENT

TO THE

SEVENTH EDITION

OF THE

Practitioner's Probate Manual.

The Practitioner's Probate Manual.

(SEVENTH EDITION.)

SUPPLEMENT

TO THE ABOVE,

SHOWING THE CHANGES EFFECTED

BY THE

LAND TRANSFER ACT, 1897,

(*60 & 61 Victoria, cap. 65.*)

AND THE

FINANCE ACT, 1900.

(*Section 13.*)

By Section 1 of the above Act it is enacted that where Real Estate is vested in any person without a right in any other person to take by survivorship it shall, on his death, notwithstanding any testamentary disposition, devolve to and become vested in his personal representatives or representative from time to time as if it were a chattel real vesting in them or him.

The Section is to apply to any Real Estate over which a person executes by Will a general power of appointment as if it were Real Estate vested in him.

Probate and Letters of Administration may be granted in respect of Real Estate only, although there is no personal Estate.

The expression " Real Estate " in this Act shall not be deemed to include land of copyhold tenure or customary freehold in any case in which an admission or any act by the Lord of the Manor is necessary to perfect the title of a purchaser from the customary tenant.

The Section applies only in cases of death after the commencement of the Act, which is the 1st day of January, 1898.

By Section 2(4) it is provided that where a person dies possessed of Real Estate the Court shall in granting Letters of Administration have regard to the rights and interests of persons interested in his Real Estate, and his heir-at-law, if not one of the next-of-kin, shall be equally entitled to the Grant with the next-of-kin. When, therefore, the applicant for the Grant is not one of the next-of-kin of the deceased, it will be necessary to show either that the deceased did not die possessed of Real Estate, or, by separate Affidavit, who is the heir-at-law. The most common case is that of an application for Grant by a guardian of a minor, when it must be shown, by separate Affidavit, that one of the minors electing the guardian, or for whose use the Grant is given, is the heir-at-law of the deceased.

The passing of this Act has necessitated a change in the forms used in the Probate Registry, and these forms are given in the following pages. The forms are available for all cases, whether the deceased died before the 1st January, 1898, or on or after that date.

The reference in the forms throughout the *Probate Manual* to the " Personal Estate and Effects of the Deceased " should be varied, so as to read, " all the Estate which by law devolves to and vests in the personal representative of the deceased."

It should be noted that in the form of Oath the amount of the Estate to be inserted will, if deceased died before 1st January, 1898, be the gross value of his personal Estate only ; but if he died on or after that date, the gross value of the personal Estate plus the gross value of the Real Estate must be given.

[*Oath for Executor.*]

(*Page 11, " Probate Manual."*)

(USUAL HEADING.)

IN the Estate of   deceased.
I (or We)   of   make oath and say, that   believe the paper
writing   hereto annexed, and marked by   to contain the true and original last Will
and Testament   of   of
formerly of   deceased, who died on the   day of   1
at   that   and that
Execut   in the said   named, and that   will well and faithfully
administer according to law all the Estate which by law devolves to and vests in the personal
representative of the said deceased, and that   will exhibit a true and perfect inventory
of the said Estate, and render a just and true account thereof, whenever required by law
so to do ; and that the gross value of the said Estate of the said deceased amounts to £ *
and no more to the best of   knowledge, information and belief.

Sworn, etc.

[*Oath for Administrator (Will).*]

(*Page 48, " Probate Manual."*)

(USUAL HEADING.)

IN the Estate of   deceased.
I (or We)   make oath and say, that   believe the paper
writing   hereto annexed, and marked by   to contain the true and original last Will
and Testament   of   of
formerly of   deceased, who died on the   day of   1
at   and that   and that   will
well and faithfully administer according to law all the Estate which by law devolves to
and vests in the personal representative of the said deceased, and that   will exhibit
a true and perfect inventory of the said Estate, and render a just and true account thereof,
whenever required by law so to do ; and that the gross value of the said Estate of the said
deceased amounts to £ *   and no more, to the best of   knowledge, information, and belief.

Sworn, etc.

[*Oath for Administrator.*]

(*Page 75, " Probate Manual."*)

(USUAL HEADING.)

IN the Estate of   deceased.
I (or We)   make oath and say, that   of
deceased, died on the   day of   1   at
Intestate a   and that
of the said deceased, that   will faithfully administer according to law all the Estate
which by law devolves to and vests in the personal representative of the said deceased ;
that   will exhibit a true and perfect inventory of the said Estate, andr end era just
and true account thereof, whenever required by law so to do ; and that the gross value of
the said Estate of the said deceased amounts to £ *   and no more, to the best
of   knowledge, information, and belief.

---

* If the deceased died on or since the 1st January, 1898, insert the *gross* value of the Personal
plus the *gross* value of the Real Estate, as defined by Sec. 1, Land Transfer Act, 1897. If
deceased died before 1st January, 1898, insert the gross value of the Personal Estate only.

[Bond—Intestacy.]

(Page 83, " Probate Manual.")

Know All Men by these Presents, that We
are jointly and severally bound unto The Right Honourable
the President of the Probate Divorce and Admiralty Division
of Her Majesty's High Court of Justice, in the Sum of *
Pounds, of good and lawful money of *Great Britain*, to be paid to the said

or to the President of the said Division for the time being, for which payment
well and truly to be made we bind ourselves and each of us for the Whole, our
Heirs, Executors and Administrators firmly by these Presents. Sealed with our
Seals. Dated the   day of   in the Year
of our Lord One Thousand Nine Hundred
The Condition of this Obligation is such, that if the above-named
the   of   of   deceased, who died on the   day of
1   and the intended Administrat   of all the Estate which by law devolves to and
vests in the personal representative of the said deceased
do, when lawfully called on in that behalf make, or cause to be made, a true and perfect
Inventory of the said Estate   which has or shall come to
                              Hands, Possession, or Knowledge, or into the Hands and Possession
of any other Person for   , and the same so made do exhibit, or cause to
be exhibited, into the   Registry of the Probate Division of Her Majesty's
High Court of Justice   , whenever required by Law so to do. And the
said Estate   do well and truly Administer according to Law. And
further do make, or cause to be made, a just and true Account of
said Administration, whenever required by Law so to do. And if it shall hereafter appear that
any last Will and Testament was made by the said Deceased, and the Executor or Executors
or other persons therein named do exhibit the same into the Probate Division of the said
Court, making request to have it allowed and approved accordingly, if the said intended
Administrat   being thereunto required, do render and deliver the Letters of Administration
(approbation of such Testament being first had and made) in the said Court, then this
Obligation to be void and of none effect, or else to remain in full force and virtue.

[Bond—Administration (Will).]

(Page 63, " Probate Manual.")

Know All Men by these Presents, That We
are jointly and severally bound unto The Right Honourable
the President of the Probate, Divorce and Admiralty Division of Her Majesty's
High Court of Justice, in the sum of *   Pounds
of good and lawful money of *Great Britain*, to be paid to the said

or to the President of the said Division for the time being, for which payment
well and truly to be made we bind ourselves and each of us, for the whole, our
Heirs, Executors and Administrators, firmly by these Presents.
Sealed with our Seals.   Dated the   day of
in the year of our Lord One Thousand Nine Hundred
The Condition of this Obligation is such, that if the above-named
of   of   , deceased, who died on the   day of   1   and the
intended Administrat   (with the Will   annexed) of all the Estate which by law
devolves to and vests in the personal representative of the said deceased
do when lawfully called on in that behalf, make or cause to be made a true and perfect Inventory of the said Estate   which has or shall come to
                    Hands, Possession, or Knowledge, and the same so made do exhibit, or cause
to be exhibited, into the   Registry of the said Division at
whenever required by law so to do, and the said Estate   do well and truly
Administer according to law, and further do make or cause to be made a just and true
Account of   said Administration when   shall be thereunto lawfully required,
then this Obligation to be void and of none effect, or else to remain in full force and virtue.

* NOTE.—If deceased died on **or** since 1st January, 1898, the Penal Sum is double the gross
Personal Estate *plus* double the gross Annual Value of the Real Estate.   If deceased
died before that date the Penal Sum is double the gross Personal Estate.

[*Declaration of Estate.*]

(*Page 133*, " *Probate Manual.*")

(USUAL HEADING.)

IN the Estate of   deceased.
A true declaration of all the Estate which by law devolves to and vests in the personal
representative of   of   deceased,
who died on the   day of   1   at   (and had at
the time of h   death a fixed place of abode at   ) which has at any time
since h   death come to the hands, possession or knowledge of
the intended Administrat   of the said Estate made and exhibited
upon and by virtue of the Corporal Oath of the said   as follows, to wit :

First, this declarant declares the said Estate to be as follows :—

Personal Property :—

	£	s.	d.

Real Property :—

	£	s.	d.

This declarant further declares that no Estate devolving to and vesting as aforesaid in the
personal representative of the said deceased has at any time since h   death come to the
hands, possession or knowledge of this declarant, save as hereinbefore set forth.

On the   day of   1
the said
was duly sworn to the truth of the
above declaration at
in the

Before me

A Commissioner for Oaths.

[*Affidavit for Notation of Domicile.*]

(*Page 134*, " *Probate Manual.*")

(USUAL HEADING.)

IN the Estate of   deceased.
I,   make Oath, and say that
of   deceased, died on the   day of
1   , at   and was at the time of h   death domiciled
in that part of the United Kingdom called England, that
granted to me by the said Court at the   Registry thereof, on the
day of   1   , that all the Estate which by Law devolves to and vests
in the personal representative of the said deceased within the United Kingdom of Great
Britain and Ireland, and for or in respect of which the said   granted,
exclusive of what the said deceased may have been possessed of or entitled to as a Trustee for
any other person or persons and not beneficially, and without deducting anything on account
of the debts due and owing from the said deceased, was of the gross value of £
to the best of my knowledge, information, and belief.

And I further make oath that a part of the said estate of the value of £
was in England, and a further part thereof amounting in value to the sum of £   ,
and more particularly mentioned and set forth in the Schedule hereunto annexed, was in
Scotland, and that the said deceased was   at the time of h   death possessed
of or entitled to   estate in Ireland
to the best of my knowledge, information, and belief.

Sworn, etc.

[Oath for Executors, including Scotch Property.]

(Page 134, " Probate Manual.")

(USUAL HEADING.)

IN the Estate of   deceased.
I (or We)   make Oath and say, that   believe the paper
writing   hereto annexed, and marked by   to contain the true and original last Will and
Testament   of   of
formerly of   deceased, who died on the   day of   1
at   that
and that   Execut   in the said   named,
and that   will well and faithfully administer according to law the Estate which by law
devolves to and vests in the personal representative of the said deceased and that   will
exhibit a true and perfect inventory of the said Estate and render a just and true account
thereof, whenever required by law so to do; that the said deceased died domiciled in
England; and that the gross value of the said Estate of the said deceased in the United
Kingdom amounts to £   and no more, to the best of   knowledge, information
and belief.

 Sworn, etc.

—

[Oath for Guardian of Minors.]

(Page 72, " Probate Manual.")

(USUAL HEADING.)

I,   of
make Oath and say, that   of
deceased, died on the   day of   at
a   and intestate leaving   h   natural and lawful
and only child   and only next-of-kin who are now in their minority   to wit
the said   a minor of the age of   years only, the
said   a minor of the age of   years only :
that there is no testamentary or other lawfully appointed guardian of the said minors
          : that   the lawful   of the said minors,
and that the said minors have by an instrument in writing bearing date the   day of
          1   , elected or chosen   to be their curator or guardian for the
purpose of taking out Letters of Administration of all the Estate which by Law devolves to
and vests in the personal representative of the said deceased to be granted to   for
                and until one of them shall attain the age of 21 years ; that   will
faithfully administer according to law all the Estate which by law devolves to and vests in
the personal representative of the said deceased for the use and benefit of the said minors
                and until one of them shall attain the age of 21 years ; that   will
exhibit a true and perfect inventory of the said Estate and render a just and true account
thereof whenever required by law so to do; and that the gross value of the said Estate of
the said deceased amounts to £   and no more, to the best of
knowledge, information, and belief.*

 Sworn, etc.

---

* If there is no real Estate add, "And I further make oath and say that the said deceased did
not die possessed of any real Estate."

9

[*Affidavit as to Heir-at-Law of Deceased.*]

(USUAL HEADING.)

In the Estate of   deceased.
I   of
make oath and say as follows:—

1. That
deceased, died on the   day of   1   , at   aforesaid,
a bachelor without a parent and intestate (*or as the case may be*).

2. That the said deceased was at the date of   death possessed of certain
freehold property, situate at   , which said real Estate
became the property of the deceased by virtue of three several Indentures of Conveyance
on a purchase of the said freehold property by the said

3. That   late of   ,
the father of the said deceased, was married once only, viz., to   ,
in or about the year   . He died on   day of   18   , having
survived his said wife

4. There were issue of the marriage   children, and no more, viz. :—

5. That under the circumstances stated in this Affidavit I am the heir-at-law of the
said deceased,

Sworn by the said
at   in the
          the   day of
                    19
Before me

A Commissioner for Oaths.

[*Renunciation of Probate and Administration (Will).*]

(*Page 137, " Probate Manual."*)

(USUAL HEADING.)

WHEREAS   of   deceased, died on the
day of   One thousand nine hundred   at
and had at the time of h   death a fixed place of abode at   within the
district of   AND WHEREAS   he made and duly executed h   last Will and
Testament,   bearing date the   day of   One thousand   hundred
and
and thereof appointed

NOW   the said   do hereby declare, that   have not intermeddled in the
Estate which by law devolves to and vests in the personal representative of the said deceased,
and will not hereafter intermeddle therein, with intent to defraud creditors ; and   do
hereby expressly renounce all   right and title to the Probate and execution of the said
Will   and to the Letters of Administration with the said Will   annexed, of
the said Estate of the said deceased.

Signed by the said, etc.

[*Renunciation of Administration.*]

(*Page 138, " Probate Manual."*)

(USUAL HEADING.)

WHEREAS   late of   in the
County of   deceased, died on the   day of
One thousand   hundred and   at
Intestate   leaving me

NOW   the said   do hereby renounce all
right and title to the Letters of Administration of the Estate which by law devolves to and
vests in the personal representative of the said deceased.

Signed, etc.

AFFIDAVIT FOR INLAND REVENUE.

In respect of the Estate of persons who have died on or after 1st January, 1898, the following forms must be used:—

Form A-3 for cases in which Form A-1 was applicable for deaths prior to 1st January, 1898 (*see* page 23 of the *Manual.*)

It should be particularly noted that in every case paragraph 7, which shows the value of the Estate in respect of which the Grant is to be given, must remain.

The Account No. 1 contains two parts, part No. 1 being for the personal Estate of the deceased, and part No. 2 containing particulars of the gross annual value and the gross principal value of the Real Estate in England vested in the deceased without a right in any other person to take by survivorship; and real property over which deceased executed by Will a general power of appointment. Copyhold or customary land, where an admission or act by the Lord of the Manor is necessary to perfect the title of a purchaser from the customary tenant, is *not* to be included in this Account No. 1.

If the duty on this Real Estate is being paid upon the Affidavit, full particulars thereof are to be given in Account No. 5; if not so paid, particulars, not necessarily in detail, should be given in a separate account.

In Account No. 5 should be given particulars of all Real Estate in respect of which Estate Duty is payable upon the death of deceased, and which duty is being paid upon the Affidavit, whether the property is aggregable or non-aggregable.

If there is any property which is chargeable with Estate Duty on the death of the deceased, but in respect of which the duty is not being paid upon the Affidavit, the particulars thereof should be shown by separate Accounts and should not be included in the Accounts Nos. 3 to 5 in the Affidavit.

Form A-4 for cases where the only property passing is Personal Estate under the deceased's Will or intestacy.

Form B-2 is for cases in which Form B-1 was applicable for deaths prior to 1st January, 1898 (*see* page 23 of the *Manual*). The form is similar to Form B-1, but makes provision for indicating the Real Estate which devolves to or vests in the personal representative of the deceased. It should be particularly noted that paragraph 6, which shows the value of the Estate in respect of which the grant is to be given, must in every case remain.

The Rules as to the description and valuation of Real Estate which are indicated on pages 32-34 of the *Manual* remain unaltered.

By Section 5 of the Land Transfer Act, 1897, it is enacted that nothing in the first part of the Act shall affect any duty payable in respect of Real Estate, or impose any other duty than is now payable in respect thereof.

By Section 13 of the Finance Act, 1900, the rate and amount of duty payable upon the Estates of persons dying on or after the 9th April, 1900, will be determined by the exact amount of the net value of the Estate.

If, therefore, the net value of the Estate of a person so dying is £509, the rate of duty will be 2 per cent., and the amount of duty will be £10 3s. 7d.

The basis for rate and amount of duty in the cases of persons dying *before* the 9th April, 1900, will be as indicated on page 35 of the *Probate Manual*.

FOR LIST OF FORMS SEE OVER.

N.B.—In every case where the death was before 1st January, 1898, the old forms of Affidavit must be used.

—WATERLOW & SONS LIMITED, LONDON WALL, LONDON. —

www.ingramcontent.com/pod-product-compliance
Lightning Source LLC
Chambersburg PA
CBHW030316270326
41926CB00010B/1396